W9-BCJ-426

TORMENTED GENIUS ▪ THE STRUGGLES OF VINCENT VAN GOGH

TORMENTED GENIUS ▪ THE STRUGGLES OF VINCENT VAN GOGH

BY ALAN HONOUR

WITH SIX FULL-COLOR PLATES

WILLIAM MORROW AND COMPANY   NEW YORK 1967

The author wishes to express his deep appreciation to Dr. V. W. van Gogh (nephew of the artist) of Rozenlaantje, The Netherlands, for his interest in this book, for his prompt and courteous assistance, and for his permission to quote from Vincent van Gogh's correspondence.

The author is also grateful to Doubleday & Company, Inc. for permission to quote from *Dear Theo, The Autobiography of Vincent van Gogh,* edited by Irving Stone, copyright 1937 by Irving Stone; to Harcourt, Brace & World, Inc. for permission to quote from *Vincent van Gogh* by Julius Meier-Graefe; to the New York Graphic Society for permission to quote from *The Complete Letters of Vincent van Gogh;* to The Museum of Modern Art, New York, for permission to quote from *Vincent van Gogh, Letters to Emile Bernard,* edited and translated by Douglas Lord; and to Random House, Inc. for permission to quote from *Passionate Pilgrim, The Life of Vincent van Gogh* by Lawrence and Elisabeth Hanson.

**FOR GEORGE, LILY,
AND
SHIRLEY HONOUR**

CONTENTS

CONTENTS

AUTHOR'S NOTE

In his lifetime Vincent van Gogh, the great painter, was ignored. Almost at the instant of his death, however, he became a legend, and controversy still surrounds this enigmatic man.

Van Gogh's life was a tragic triumph. Through his art he achieved immortality; as a man he was a failure, for he never learned to control his emotions. Bitterness and sorrow were his friends, and we can only wonder at the suffering a human being can stand before breaking. Without doubt, this gifted artist was one of the loneliest men who ever lived.

Existing on a slender income, van Gogh very occasionally added to it with the sale of a drawing or two. Although his canvases are now worth fortunes, he sold only one of his paintings—and that for a paltry four hundred francs.

The story of Vincent van Gogh is properly the story of two men, for without his younger brother Theo it is likely there would be none to tell. Vincent wrote hundreds of letters, the bulk of them addressed to his brother. Written in Dutch, French, English, and often a mixture of all three, they are difficult to translate. At times they are poorly constructed, for he put down his ideas just as they flitted about in his mind. Yet this collection forms one of the world's most remarkable documents, in which van Gogh holds a mirror to himself such as few men ever have.

In his letters van Gogh records a tragedy that ranks with the world's greatest. In his paintings and drawings he records a truth and beauty that will live forever.

Alan Honour
Richmond, Indiana

1 A TROUBLED BEGINNING ▪

The little village of Zundert is in Holland, in the Brabant district not far from the border of Belgium. Before the coming of railways, Zundert was a regular stopping place for stagecoaches passing between Amsterdam and Paris. The only time the village seemed much alive was when the cobbled streets echoed with the rattle of the stagecoach arriving or departing.

In 1849, an attractive young man was inducted as pastor of a village church in Zundert. Twenty-seven-year-old Theodorus van Gogh, then a bachelor, had a good deal of charm and was soon widely known as "the handsome pastor." Well liked by his neighbors and his congregation, he was somewhat rigid and formal in manner, yet not without kindness. Although he lacked real depth of understanding, he gave of his worldly goods to those in need, and this strong sense of duty toward his fellow men was a softening touch.

For two years Theodorus van Gogh lived alone in the parsonage. Then at the age of twenty-nine he married Anna Cornelia Carbentus, a woman three years older than himself. Mrs. van Gogh had many good qualities. She was a sensible wife and house-keeper, attentive to her husband's parishioners, and she had a fine talent for drawing and watercolor painting. Her studies of flower arrangements were exquisite in detail and color tones.

Early in 1852, the van Goghs thought their happiness was to be crowned by an event they both desired with all their hearts. On the thirtieth of March Anna van Gogh gave birth to a son; alas, the child was born dead. After the birth was registered, she picked a spot in the churchyard at Zundert, and, perhaps in an effort to ease her mind, she insisted on having an unusually large and expensive stone put over the grave. The dead child had been named Vincent, for his grandfather.

Mrs. van Gogh took her loss very hard, and the warm atmosphere of the parsonage changed abruptly to one of gloom and mourning. Torn by feelings of guilt and doubt, she wondered whether it was her fault the child had not lived. Anna van Gogh simply could not forget the dead child, and she became unreasonable in her grief. Brooding over her tragedy, she often sat in silence for long periods, tears trickling down her plump cheeks. And she was growing into an extremely irritable person.

The pastor loved his wife, but he had little real assistance to offer her. The idea that perhaps God did not intend his children to suffer did not seem to occur to him. He advocated upright living, which meant that one must "suffer the slings and arrows of outrageous fortune" in silence and meek subservience. For a man fiercely and sincerely dedicated to leading souls to salvation, he had remarkably little understanding of the passions and hungers of the souls he sought to save.

In the early months of 1853 it was obvious that Anna was again to bear a child. She took no joy in the prospect, however, as she was fearful that the event might be a repetition of the previous birth. Still she lashed herself with thoughts that the loss of the first child was in some mysterious way a punishment upon her. What should have been a happy time was instead a period of gloomy foreboding.

On March 30, 1853 Anna bore another son. The baby was obviously a van Gogh—he had their red hair and freckles—but his deep-set, blue-green eyes were just like his mother's. He drew his first breath of life on the same day as the birth, one year earlier, of the dead Vincent. The number of the birth certificate was twenty-nine—the same as that of the first child's —and his parents named him Vincent, also.

Very soon, other children followed Vincent into the family. When he was two years old, sister Anna arrived. She was followed by Theo, Elizabeth, Wilhelmien, and later a younger brother Cornelius, whom they all called Cor.

By the time he was able to walk, Vincent was already a lonely, isolated little boy. Apparently his mother did not like the child who had taken the place of her firstborn, and she showed no true warmth toward him. Fully occupied, Anna van Gogh overlooked her child's needs and refused to participate in his discovery of the wonders of the world about him. The pastor was usually too busy with the affairs of his parish, except at mealtimes, for any real closeness with his son. Knowing he was not really liked by either of his parents caused the child to develop deep feelings of rejection, and the more he tried to get close to his parents, the deeper the feelings of rejection became, for their remote attitude did not change. Furthermore, his mother's frequent reference to the dead child was deeply disturbing to van Gogh, planting in the boy the guilty feeling that he was a usurper.

Vincent van Gogh was an ugly little boy, and as time passed he began to develop his mother's quick temper and nervousness, becoming as emotional and unreasoning as she. Usually ensconced in his study, the pastor seldom paid much attention, but van Gogh began to grow extremely defiant of his mother. The more she scolded, the more he took a perverse delight in doing the things that brought reprimands upon his head. His disposition did not improve when his sisters, taking a cue from their mother, added their teasing to the constant quarrels.

Sunday morning was always a special time in the van Gogh home. Off to the cemetery Madame van Gogh marched her brood, each carrying a small bunch of flowers. At the graveyard the small procession gathered around a gravestone, looking solemn under the stern face of their mother. Vincent van Gogh could not help but read his own name inscribed on the stone.

The one relief from the Sunday mornings was the church service. To van Gogh, his godlike father's sermons were beautiful, and they awoke in the boy a wonderment about God. Stories of the words and actions of Jesus and his gentle and sweet ways penetrated deeply into his soul. Van Gogh thought his handsome father looked like a saint. His one hope and dream was to become as good, upright, and fine as he was.

He also enjoyed the times when his father took him along on errands of mercy in poor and shabby homes. Vincent van Gogh vowed, over and over again, that one day he, too, would do God's work. Entering the ministry would be his goal in life.

A streak of fanaticism appearing throughout the generations of the van Gogh famliy took the form of the notion of duty and service to one's fellow men. Family members never *worked* at professions; they always *served* as teachers, art dealers, or pastors. Thus, from the very beginning, this idea was drummed into van Gogh's mind.

Every adult who knew van Gogh commented on his strangeness. Already an outcast in his own home, the withdrawn and lonely boy trudged miles into the countryside at every opportunity. There he found a world full of new delights, which he could enjoy in peace. At least, no one denied him the pleasures that nature offered so freely.

Away from the parsonage the unhappy boy forgot his troubles. He delighted in everything he noticed and found life a miraculous thing. The behavior of birds captivated him; he loved observing their flight and sometimes found a secluded spot where he spent hours watching a bird feed its young. He examined their nests, astonished at the intricate intertwining of the grasses and twigs and at the coloring and markings of the eggs.

Van Gogh knew and loved the country around Zundert in all its moods and seasons. Watching farmers plough, sow, and reap, he came to love these simple folk, who were close to the earth. When he was studying an insect on the ground or climbing a tree to look closely at the pattern of its leaves, nature spoke with a clear voice to the lonely boy, and his soul listened. There was no human voice to help the boy examine and understand his thoughts properly.

Careless of his clothes, he often returned home from

these excursions into the country with something torn or badly soiled, and his parents' nagging resumed. Had the pastor known his son's behavior during these absences, he might have been less troubled by him.

Feeling rejected in his home, van Gogh also wandered into the village. In the homes of some of the boys he knew he did not feel unwanted. They paid no attention to his clothes, since most of them had only those that they wore. He loved these uncomplicated people and tried to model himself upon them. And as his awareness grew, anger at the stark poverty of their lives began to grow.

With birds and animals and with those few people he liked, van Gogh could be gentleness itself. In his home there was peace only when he was absorbed with pencil and paper, pen and ink. He had a passion to draw and was becoming good at it. This pastime calmed him, but his mother, despite her own fine ability at drawing, seldom offered any help or advice. Van Gogh began to carry drawing materials in his pockets and stopped his wandering whenever something unusual caught his attention, trying to capture it with his pencil on paper.

Theo, now five years old, worshiped Vincent and was becoming very important to him. From his brother, who gave his love so freely, van Gogh took comfort. Young as he was, Theo van Gogh was often able to soothe his troubled heart. The boys grew so close that, in order to stay together as much as possi-

ble, they even shared a bed. It was a great delight
when they were both allowed to accompany their father on his walks and errands.

By this point van Gogh took a positive delight in
being dirty, untidy, and clumsy. The disturbed boy's
manner of speech reflected the conflict within him.
Constant misunderstanding, the choking back of swift
anger made him talk in an odd, rough-sounding series
of spasms. Just to be difficult, he often refused to conform, not caring even when his beloved father looked
at him disdainfully. He comforted himself with the
knowledge that his brother loved him anyway; Theo
never complained to their mother about him, and he
never mocked him for being dirty. Therefore, Theo
became the only one worthy to share his older brother's secrets and discoveries.

No matter how van Gogh looked most of the time,
his mother always had him sparkling clean for visits
from Uncle Vincent, who lived in a big house at
Prinsenhage. Uncle Vincent was an art dealer and a
jolly man. He did not seem to notice his nephew's
uncouth speech, clumsiness, or unattractiveness; he
liked his namesake and took an interest in him.

On return visits to Prinsenhage, young van Gogh
enjoyed studying the paintings in his uncle's house.
The colors fascinated him, and he was especially
pleased with those that pictured the peasants of the
countryside or made use of a religious motif. While
looking at the paintings, the ugly duckling was, for a
while, content. Van Gogh met some of his uncle's

friends and clients, too, and these contacts made him aware of the great world beyond Zundert.

As he grew older, van Gogh's life at the parsonage did not improve. He insisted on keeping company with rough village boys and was almost indifferent to his mother's entreaties. In his unhappiness his anger often became uncontrollable, and he was impossible to handle.

In 1864, eleven-year-old Vincent van Gogh was sent to a boarding school that trained and educated young gentlemen. The boy was not particularly interested in going, but he had no complaint about this decision. Perhaps the thought of living away from home all the time attracted him.

It was a cold, wet day when his parents took him to Zevenbergen, and van Gogh became as gloomy as the weather. He wavered between a desire to run away and a desire to find out what this new experience would bring. Nevertheless, he resolved to be good at school. He would pay attention and study hard, and he would not make trouble for anyone. When he returned home his parents would be proud of him. With his father's help, he would become a good pastor, too, in the service of God.

After his mother's final admonitions about keeping neat and clean, van Gogh found himself alone in the new school. He was quickly sensitive to the fact that his appearance was loutish compared to that of the other boys. Although he made an effort to be pleasant whenever someone spoke to him, he was suspicious of adults, and he looked at people in a sly, sidewise fashion instead of straight in the face. His speech was now almost a stammer, which further handicapped him.

At first the boy made efforts to be friendly and to gain acceptance, but he soon found out that he had little in common with most of the other students. He tried to show an interest in what they found important, but they expressed none in his love of nature or his skill with a pencil. Once when he tried a sketch of another boy his effort was laughed at. If anyone offered a touch of warmth, young van Gogh responded overeagerly, which together with his odd speech and peculiar characteristics generally discouraged the other boy from forming a friendship. More and more van Gogh felt alone and acted accordingly, becoming surly and morose. All his efforts to be friendly proved futile, because most of the other boys found him repulsive.

At mealtimes he began to notice that some of the boys were making fun of him. As a result, he refused to eat with them. He waited his turn to be served, then without a comment or a glance at his classmates he marched to the far end of the room. There in a corner he ate his food, silent and alone. If he overheard the boys' snickering, he turned and glared in their direction. His blue eyes flashed, and his red hair seemed to turn redder and almost bristle. So fierce could he appear that the other boys eventually left him utterly alone.

Nursing his sense of failure, young van Gogh plodded through five years at the school in Zevenbergen. In that time he did not make a single close friend. However, he acquired the love of good books. His greatest pleasure became reading, which offered him many friends and new worlds to explore. Perhaps this reading gave him his education, for he never developed the ability to study patiently.

School failed to teach van Gogh discipline or self-control. In class he was argumentative and quarreled with his teachers and other students. He questioned everything and refused to accept an explanation unless it suited his own thinking. Though he managed to keep up with his lessons, they bored him on the whole.

On the other hand, van Gogh's interest in drawing continued to develop. Sometimes he missed classes because he had been completely lost in sketching whatever had absorbed him at the moment. Since his absences from class were a relief, nobody reported him. If he were chastised, however, his temper flashed, for he never recognized that he might deserve the reprimand.

School did not soften his wild nature, and this new rejection pushed him back into the careless and dirty habits his mother, with some justice, complained of so often and so bitterly. In his misery van Gogh failed completely to discover that he caused many of his difficulties himself.

When, in 1869, he left the school at the age of sixteen, van Gogh had turned inward so much that he had become a boor. Narrow-minded in his attitudes and tastes, he sometimes sounded like a man four times his age. His blunt rudeness drove others away from him, and if someone offered him a friendly hand he refused the gesture no matter what the motive. Van Gogh was trapped in the vicious circle of his own tortured feelings. Loneliness made him harsh, and his harshness fed his loneliness.

Throughout his school years the vision van Gogh had of his father stayed with him. Yet he did not recognize that his inability to get along with others would prevent him from following in his father's footsteps, much as he desired to do so. He began to believe that only by suffering would he learn, and he almost welcomed his tormented thoughts. Longing to serve his fellow men as his father did, he vowed to himself that his life, which he sometimes thought was his by default, would be lived nobly.

The inconsistencies of his thinking, affected by reading too many books he did not understand wholly, escaped his notice. With this confusing mixture of beliefs and ideas, and no regrets for the school, Vincent van Gogh returned to his parents.

2 ■ THE YOUNG ART DEALER

Except for Theo, the family expressed little joy or welcome when van Gogh arrived home. Apparently the pastor and his wife found his behavior more defiant and hostile than ever. At sixteen, van Gogh was callow and without attainments. Constantly he told himself how much he loved his fellow men and how sincerely he wanted to serve them. Nevertheless, despite this professed love, he appeared to be completely unfeeling about the few people close to him, especially his parents.

At the same time young van Gogh was beginning to have vague feelings that perhaps he had some special power within himself. He idly dreamed of following his father's footsteps. But how? His parents gave him no encouragement. That he had made no preparations for such a course and more or less thrown away the opportunity his schooling might have provided meant nothing to him.

Vincent van Gogh's desire to become a pastor like his father was ignored. Instead, the hopes of his mother were realized. Mrs. van Gogh wished to see her son safely settled in a sound profession, and Uncle Vincent had important interests in Goupil's, a respected and highly prosperous art gallery. He arranged for his nephew to go to work there at The Hague.

Oddly enough young van Gogh made no protest. Possibly he felt relieved that the decision had been made for him. He loved paintings and, except for missing Theo's company, he had no regrets at leaving the parsonage again. In midsummer of 1869, van Gogh started work, and big-city living temporarily stilled the struggling and torment he had always known. There was so much going on around him, and it was all new. The Hague seemed enormous compared to the few places he had seen. Everywhere there was noise, color, and bustle, and each day was different. Goupil's sold prints of famous paintings and original works of art of all kinds. Young van Gogh liked best the Dutch painters, whose somber pictures called to the somber spirit that was his own. As his heroes he chose men like Mesdag, Joseph Israels, and Jean François Millet. From these painters he believed he caught an echo of the beautiful, the simple, the good—all of which he hoped to build into his own life.

At The Hague van Gogh remained an awkward, coarse-looking young man, but he lost the desire to look like a peasant. He dressed neatly and kept himself tidy. He discovered, too, that the van Goghs were indeed an honored family and a very close one. His uncle and other members of the family tried to teach him everything they knew about the business.

Slowly at first, a regular correspondence began between Vincent and Theo van Gogh, one that continued throughout their lives. Vincent, who still had great difficulty making himself clear in his speech or in his writing, started the habit of enclosing sketches in his letters to tell his brother what he could not describe in words. Trying to instruct his younger brother and influence him over the years, Vincent van Gogh revealed much of the confusion of his thoughts in these letters. The correspondence is a fascinating record of his feelings and actions and of his beloved brother's efforts to help him.

Although van Gogh worked in art galleries for several years and was fascinated by paintings, he was unable to recognize his own gifts. Stubbornly he clung to the belief that he had to become a preacher. Yet his letters to Theo constantly urged him to stay close to art.

I see that you have a great love for art; that is a good thing, lad. Admire as much as you can; most people do not admire enough.

You must try by all means to get a good knowledge of pictures. Go to the museum as often as you can and keep your love for nature, for that is the true way to learn to understand art more and more. Painters understand nature and love her and teach us to see her. If one really loves nature, one can find beauty everywhere.

In one of his letters Theo informed his brother of a change in their father's status. Pastor van Gogh had accepted a call to a new church at Helvoirt, a somewhat larger village not far from Zundert. This news again stirred van Gogh's longing to become a minister, but he stayed with his job. Otherwise, the move apparently had little effect on him. He loved the country around Zundert, but the parsonage itself was filled with bitter recollections and few were the happy thoughts he had of the place.

A mood of quiet peacefulness possessed van Gogh at the moment. He loved selling the work of the painters he worshiped. Still no thought occurred to him that he might train his own talent. His taste was totally undeveloped, and he liked best the sentimental Victorian pictures that sold so well. Rich patrons, from the comfort of their many-servanted homes, idealized the simple country life and fed these daydreams with the art they purchased. The smoke and grime and slavery of the early days of industrialization offended their delicate noses, so those artists who fulfilled this desire for a clean life were the popular ones. Farm scenes, with animals and peasants working in the fields, sold well, a fact that strengthened van Gogh's belief in the simple life. In addition, he regarded the creators of such pictures as prophets. After all, didn't they create the true values of God's desires for His world for all to see? Van Gogh often lost his temper when he heard somebody criticize one of his newfound heroes.

The Angelus by Millet, young van Gogh believed, was the most beautiful painting he had ever seen; *The Sower,* he thought profound. These pictures were simple, and in them he perhaps found relief from the intense complications of his own inner feelings, which were more and more dominated by his confused concern with religion. That backbreaking drudgery could also be read into such pictures passed unnoted. Furthermore, some of these paintings brought prices as high as works by Rembrandt. "Doesn't that prove their creators are true masters?" van Gogh demanded.

Naturally, being a van Gogh, Vincent was treated well at Goupil's. If the other employees thought him a strange-looking fellow, they kept the opinion to themselves. Although they talked behind his back, they were pleasant and congenial in his presence. Still, some of his comments and actions could hardly be expected to please his employers, for van Gogh was as opinionated as ever. He was caught several times trying to talk a customer out of buying what he wanted. Often van Gogh tried to push his own favorites, but Goupil's did not consider itself a taste maker. The gallery was in business to please its clients and provide what they wanted. Van Gogh criticized the whole business of art dealing, saying that it was parasitical, paying struggling artists a pittance for works from which the gallery made handsome profits. So far, however, no great explosion had occurred.

The Hague had many delights for van Gogh. He loved to walk, and he soon knew every lane and byway of the city and the countryside beyond. His Aunt Sophie Carbentus was kind, too, and she often invited him to her big house. There, with her two daughters, he found a paradise. The painter Anton Mauve often called, and they had long discussions about painting and religion.

All the new impressions did not develop van Gogh's sense of humor, a quality he seemed to have been born without. Even at Aunt Sophie's his share in the conversations was intensely serious. He listened to the talk almost grimly and made his own points ardently. Still, everyone thought he was doing well at his work, and that was what really mattered. At least, he was very enthusiastic about selling those paintings *he* liked.

Young van Gogh was, in a fashion, happy. Although his relationships with others were shallow, he did not feel quite so lonely in the bustle of the city. Some of the guilders he earned he spent on prints of his favorite artists, which he pinned on the walls of his comfortable room on Lange Beestenmarkt. He began to buy books, reading the Bible and socially inclined writers like Charles Dickens, and to attend classes in Bible instruction. And always he walked.

Nevertheless, van Gogh remained an unattractive young man. The squareness of his head, his glittering blue eyes, and his spasmodic speech repulsed people. Being alone too much was not good for him either. The intense Bible reading and the supposedly profound ideas he had discovered in certain paintings had an adverse effect upon him. More and more, he began to feel he had some special secret power within himself. The belief was becoming almost an obsession, and the young man was oblivious to the danger. There was no one close enough to him to warn him.

In August, 1872, van Gogh had a wonderful surprise. His fifteen-year-old brother Theo, who had grown into a handsome boy much like his father, visited him. Theo was intelligent and alert, and he already knew a great deal about art. Unlike Vincent, he profited from his education, yet he suffered from it, too. He had never been strong physically, and walking ten miles to school each day took a heavy toll of his strength.

When he met Theo, van Gogh seized his hand eagerly and placed an arm about his shoulders with affection. Adopting a pose of worldly wisdom, he led his brother to his room to show him his treasures. He commented on how much Theo had grown and how strongly he resembled their father.

Observing his younger brother, van Gogh was filled

with delight. They had always been close, but they had not seen each other for a long time. Vincent saw that Theo was extremely intelligent, and he developed a new respect for him. The young men went to all the museums and art galleries, van Gogh anxiously watching his brother's reactions, seeking signs that Theo agreed with his own evaluation of the works of art they studied. One Sunday van Gogh suggested they go to the country. He wanted to show his brother one of his very favorite places.

Crossing the fields they followed a towpath beside the canal and made their way to Ryswyk. The brothers were in high spirits, but soon it started to rain. Spotting a big Dutch mill, its huge blades turning slowly in the breeze, they raced toward its shelter. Laughing and shaking the rain off their clothes, they stood just inside the door to wait for the shower to stop.

Van Gogh looked at his brother—the only human being who really cared for him—and suddenly he began to talk as he had never talked before. His closeness with Theo made him pour out the unspoken secrets of his troubled soul that had been buried so long inside him. In this very intimate moment, when he felt no embarrassment or self-consciousness, his affection for his brother released a torrent of words.

Like a conspirator, van Gogh told Theo of his deepest secret. He explained that for some years he had had a feeling that was growing stronger. Within himself, he believed, he had some strange power that had been given to him by God. But he did not know what it was and, if he found it, how was he to use it to serve humanity? He told his brother of his desire to become a preacher, explaining that because of his unique knowledge of God's desire for the course of his life he was not like other men.

Theo van Gogh was a practical boy. Young as he was and lacking in experience, he appears to have been skeptical of the tale his brother told him. He knew Vincent had no training for the ministry, and he also knew from their father's own struggles that such a life of self-denial was far from easy. In addition, Vincent seldom got along with other people for very long, especially if they did not accept his point of view. But what was he to say?

Theo's answer was to try to lead his brother away from talk of the Bible and preaching. Hopefully, he reminded van Gogh how he always appended sketches to his letters, because they described so much better than any words he commanded what he was seeing and feeling. He reminded his brother a little timidly that preachers need a vast vocabulary in order to create their lessons and sermons. Without belaboring the issue, Theo pointed out that The Hague was a leading art center and that Vincent must have met many artists since he had lived there. Couldn't he study with one of them? Surely he could learn what he had to know in order to become an artist.

Van Gogh interrupted his brother's comments impatiently and brushed them aside. He said that he felt his scribblings were much too inadequate; just thinking about them made him angry. He did not mind so much selling the works of men he considered great painters with something to tell the world. But he believed it would be presumptuous, almost a sacrilege, for him to try to become one of them. He had not the gift of poetry that he found in his favorite paintings.

Stifling his doubts in the face of his older brother's strong conviction, Theo agreed that perhaps he then should attempt to follow the ministry if his heart was set on it.

All too soon the time came for Theo to return to Helvoirt. Van Gogh watched him pack his few belongings with mixed feelings. He was happy to have such a loving ally, yet sad because his brother had to go back home.

This reunion with Theo made a deep impression on Vincent van Gogh. Often in his letters he referred to the episode:

What pleasant days we spent together at The Hague! I think so often of that walk on the Ryswyk road, where we drank milk after the rain, at the mill. That road of Ryswyk holds memories for me which are perhaps the most beautiful I have.

3 URSULA LOYER ∎

Shortly after his twentieth birthday van Gogh was transferred to London. Goupil's London branch supplied other art dealers, so he had little to do with the general public, which he found a pleasant relief. People who did not like his artist heroes he thought were barbarians, and too much of what he was supposed to sell he considered trash.

At the same time Theo started working at Goupil's in Brussels. Thus, another link was forged in the chain that bound the two brothers.

Traveling to London via Brussels and Paris, van Gogh met Theo at the station in Brussels, and they talked for a few minutes. When the train stopped at Paris, the young art dealer feasted his eyes upon its wonders. Paris was the largest city he had ever seen.

Nevertheless, London awed him, and he fell in love with the city.

Londoners are among the world's most considerate and polite people, and this attitude of courtesy toward strangers made van Gogh feel at home. The streets he walked were alive with people and heavy wagons drawn by great shire horses with large, shaggy feet and tinkling silver trimmings on their harness. Victorias, hackney cabs, vehicles of all sorts wove their way in and out of traffic in a bewildering pattern, and the sound of clanging bells that signaled horse-drawn buses to move on to the next stop could be heard everywhere. Most of all he liked the London street cries, especially those of the brightly dressed gypsy women, who walked the streets with baskets of sweet-smelling lavender, singing of the product they had to sell.

In search of these peddlers, van Gogh took to roaming the back streets. There he heard the man with a grindstone mounted on one wheel crying, "Knives to grind, scissors to mend." Ringing a bell, the muffin man walked up and down the streets with a flat tray, covered with a green baize cloth, upon his head. People came from their houses to purchase the flat, round, doughy delicacy he carried. The muffins were toasted and, dripping with butter, served at Sunday afternoon teas. Usually not far behind the muffin man was a fishmonger, pushing his two-wheeled barrow, piled with pink shrimp, black periwinkles, and sometimes cockles and mussels, down the middle of the street. Van Gogh especially liked his short, abrupt song of "Shrimps and winkles, winkles and shrimps."

In some ways Sundays were even more enjoyable, for the streets were quieter. Van Gogh soon discovered the Sunday morning street markets, where he came upon another face of London. He was astonished to see, in side alleys of these markets, women with piles of cast-off clothing and shoes, their wares spread on a cloth on the pavement. Crowds of London's poor surrounded these piles of clothes, picking them over to find a bargain. The sight saddened van Gogh, and he vowed again to serve God and do what he could to help the poor.

In London van Gogh earned more money and enjoyed more leisure time, too. Happily, London had so much to show him that, at first, he had little time for brooding or to be bored. He bought himself a black suit and crowned his head with a black silk top hat. The outfit was unbecoming at best, but he thought it was the proper business attire for a rising young art dealer. He made a peculiar sight walking the streets, his vividly red hair contrasting with his rusty black suit and hat. Many a startled look was cast at him, but he did not notice.

As usual van Gogh made no friends. Whenever the weather was good and he had time, he was off alone on some excursion or other. He knew all the art galleries and museums of London. Sometimes he wan-

dered out to Henry the Eighth's palace at Hampton
Court. Once he walked all the way to Brighton, a
seaside town over fifty miles from London.

But his favorite place was along the embankment
of the River Thames. On his way home from work he
began to dally, penciling scenes on his sketch paper of
the river and the buildings along its banks. The river,
which was never still and never the same any two
successive evenings, fascinated van Gogh. As the sun
went down, the golden pinks turned to a deep red,
then violet shadows and blue shadings colored dark
places. Van Gogh enjoyed watching the play of these
colors immensely. Sometimes the river was somber
and, even in these moods, he enjoyed looking at it for
hours. The changes of light on the walls of ancient
Westminster Abbey and the astonishing stonework
inside, looking more like filmy lacework than stone,
also intrigued him. Even on the brightest days the
ancient building had a permanently blue tone, for
there were parts of the structure that sunlight had not
touched in hundreds of years. Rain and fog, too, had
given this building a unique character.

Van Gogh poured out his impressions to his brother
along with sketch after sketch to illustrate his words.
He was making more drawings than ever before.

Even though he lived frugally London was very
expensive. Wanting to buy more books and prints, he
decided he would have to find cheaper lodgings, so he
moved into new quarters. After the first excitement of

London wore off, van Gogh settled into a dreary routine. He read his Bible avidly and went often to church. Occasionally he bought a few English prints for his room and books, preferably ones by philosophers whose views coincided with his own.

Van Gogh sensed immediately that his new lodgings had a real home atmosphere. The establishment was also a boarding school for a few boys. Madame Loyer, the owner, and her daughter Ursula were French, and they were kind, sympathetic people.

Before he realized it, van Gogh became a part of the family. The Loyers ignored his strange manner of dress and his unattractiveness, and Ursula often did little things that pleased him. Having people to talk with in the evening was good. He helped mark the boys' lessons, took them for walks, and planted the school's small garden. Although he still made sketches on his return from work each evening, he hurried to the warmth and comfort of his home.

In this happiness the old devils of doubt and fear almost disappeared. These people accepted *him*. His letters were full of praise for the Loyers.

Oh, Lad, I should like to have you here to show you my new lodgings. I now have a room such as I always longed for. I live with a very amusing family; they keep a school for little boys.

I am quite contented; I walk much, the neighborhood where I live is quiet, pleasant, and fresh, and I was really very lucky in finding it.

Of late I took up drawing again, but stopped.
Perhaps I shall take it up again some day or other.

Ursula was the first woman van Gogh had really
known, and he began to study her and think about
her more and more. Before long he had deluded himself that he was in love with this saintly creature. He
had difficulty in expressing his feelings at the best of
times, but in this situation it was utterly impossible
for him to declare his love.

In Ursula Loyer van Gogh thought he had found
the perfect girl: one who was noble, kind, and good.
He must find a way to tell her he loved her! But when
they walked out together, he was always too nervous
to come to the point. He began to imagine that certain small glances, comments, and attentions from
Ursula indicated she might be thinking of him as he
did of her.

And thus life drifted along until the summer of
1874 when van Gogh, now twenty-one years old, was
due to take his first holiday. The thought of going
home and leaving Ursula with his love unspoken was
more than he could bear. He dithered for days in a
fever of confusion. Finally, in his usual abrupt, impul-
sive way, he cornered Ursula and poured out a torrent
of words of love. She was shocked and rejected him
coldly. The monstrous edifice, which he had built on
Ursula's small kindnesses and expressions of sympathy, crashed about him.

Once he had made up his mind, however, van Gogh

pursued Ursula fanatically. He would not accept no
as her answer. Ursula became very annoyed with his
constant pestering. Finally, her patience exhausted,
she turned on van Gogh furiously and told him to
stop his senseless ravings. Ursula complained to her
mother, who soon told van Gogh it would be better if
he found lodgings elsewhere and kept away from her
daughter.

When van Gogh reached home his family was
shocked by his appearance. His red hair was
cropped close to his head, and the flesh was drawn
tightly over the prominent cheekbones, making his
face look like a skull. Finally the family managed to
discover what had happened. But despite all their
efforts to talk to him and to cheer him, they found van
Gogh beyond the reach of reason.

After he had told them about Ursula's refusal, van
Gogh refused to speak to anybody with other than a
grunt. When his parents tried to show sympathy, he
brushed their efforts aside. He believed his life was
broken, and he wanted none of their pious sermons.
Most of his time he spent idly sketching.

The torturous vacation was soon over, and he had to
return to his job in London. His parents were fearful
of letting him go back to England alone, so they decided that his sister Anna should accompany him. A
position was found where Anna could serve as a
French teacher at a girl's school in Welwyn. Van
Gogh knew that Madame Loyer would not change
her mind about sending him away, so he moved into

new lodgings. Sometimes the unhappy young man walked in the old neighborhood, hoping to catch a glimpse of Ursula, but to no avail.

This new blow of rejection deeply affected van Gogh. His temperament became worse than ever before. With his business acquaintances he was rude, pompous, and disagreeable. As soon as the day's work ended, he shut himself in his room to sketch and read his Bible. Anna's letters home were full of concern with what her brother was doing to himself. Finally, his mother took matters into her own hands. She talked to Uncle Vincent about his nephew, and he agreed to arrange for van Gogh to work in the Paris gallery for a while.

When van Gogh discovered his mother's interference, he was furious. He refused to write home and, in a rage, decided to ignore his parents completely forever. Even Theo van Gogh's pleading that this behavior was cruel did not touch him.

At the end of two months he was sent back to London. There, it was quickly discovered, his disposition had not improved. Wallowing in sorrow and self-pity, van Gogh found his only comforts were the Bible and his brother's letters. With Theo's help, however, he slowly, painfully got past the gloomiest of his thoughts, and hope began to revive. Unselfishness, service to God—there lay the answer. Somehow he would find a way; he would preach the word.

4 · FIRST SERMON

Vincent van Gogh's employer in London could not tolerate the situation any longer. Whenever he tried to discuss his employee's lack of interest, the poor results of his halfhearted efforts, the young man berated him. Van Gogh refused to listen, turning upon his employer with fury one time, remaining silent the next, afraid of the temperament he could hardly control. Uncle Vincent, tired of complaints, knew that something had to be done, so he again recalled his nephew to Paris. Paris is a second home for outcasts and exiles from all over the world, but its magic could not dispel van Gogh's black mood.

A young Englishman who came to Goupil's to learn the business of operating an art gallery provided an outlet for some of van Gogh's verbal passions, and he

sought the boy's company frequently. This English
boy also lived in the house where van Gogh lodged.
He took him to all the churches he knew, constantly
urging him to study the Bible. They prayed together.
And a priggish van Gogh filled the boy's mind with
his own ideas of what was good and what was not
good in art. As he was inexperienced and a stranger in
a strange land, the Englishman accepted everything
and proved a willing sounding board for van Gogh's
ideas.

More and more the type of work the gallery sold
offended van Gogh. As Christmas, 1875, drew near,
he felt he could not stay any longer, and impulsively
he took a leave of absence from his job without men-
tioning it to anyone. When he discovered his nephew's action, Uncle Vincent was furious. Though it
was the busiest time of the year at Goupil's, van Gogh
did not care very much. He set out for Etten, a remote village in the Brabant countryside to which his
father had recently moved.

After a visit with his parents, van Gogh returned to
Paris, but he was determined not to work at Goupil's.
It was just as well that he had come to this conclusion. When he got back, he no longer had his old job.
The gallery, however, was generous and, probably at
his uncle's insistence, gave him several months to find
another position.

Van Gogh thought he might like to return to England, so he answered advertisements for jobs in that
country. He still saw his English friend and together

they enlarged their studies, adding John Keats, George Eliot, and Hans Christian Andersen to their favorites. He liked the gallery no more now than he had before going home.

Things exploded when he quarreled violently one day with the manager, and he left before his few months of grace were up. Van Gogh never worked in an art gallery again.

On the same day that he left, he received an answer to one of his job inquiries. Mr. Stokes, principal of a school for boys in Ramsgate, a seaside holiday town in the southeast corner of England, offered van Gogh a month's trial. He was to help teach the boys elementary mathematics, French, and German. Overjoyed, van Gogh felt sure that this opportunity was a sign from heaven, and all his problems, as if by magic, seemed to vanish. In late spring of 1876, he set out for his new job.

At first everything pleased him. Van Gogh liked the gracious-looking house, which had a short flight of steps leading to the front door, a second-floor veranda overlooking the ocean, and a large bay window that lent elegance to the front on the street. He did not even complain when he found the place infested with bugs. Furthermore, he got along well with Mr. Stokes and the other teacher, and he liked the few dozen boys who lived there, often taking them for walks along the beaches.

Before long van Gogh discovered that Mr. Stokes could be a very stubborn man. When he was in a

rage, everybody felt the sting of his mood. The
month's trial soon ended, and still Mr. Stokes had
made no mention of any salary or the future. Van
Gogh did not know if he was to be kept in his position
or not. When he brought the matter up with his employer, Mr. Stokes told van Gogh that the school was
moving to a new location at Ilseworth near London
and that if he cared to come and discuss the matter
when they were settled there, something might be
decided.

Van Gogh had very little money left, and Mr.
Stokes could not pay his fare to London, so he walked
all the long way from Ramsgate. Telling his brother
of the experience he said little of the great stamina
the long walk must have required of him.

Last Monday I started from Ramsgate to London; it is a long walk and when I left, it was very
hot and it stayed so until the evening when I arrived in Canterbury. That same evening I went still
a little farther, till I arrived at a few large beech
and elm trees near a little pond where I rested for a
while. At half-past three in the morning the birds
began to sing at sight of dawn and I started again.
It was fine to walk then.

In the afternoon I arrived at Chatham, where
one sees in the distance between partly flooded low
meadows, with elm trees here and there, the Thames
full of ships; I believe it is always gray weather
there. At Chatham a cart took me a few miles far-

ther, but then the driver went into an inn, so I continued my way and arrived towards evening in the familiar suburbs of London and walked to the city along the long, long roads.

On the way van Gogh stopped at Welwyn, just outside London, and visited his sister Anna. There was little that she could offer her brother by way of money or comfort.

As soon as the school was settled in its new home, van Gogh asked once again about his salary and his future with Mr. Stokes. Things were not going well, and Mr. Stokes abruptly told him that he could not afford the salary of another teacher. He reminded van Gogh that many young men were willing to take the job for just their board and lodging.

Mr. Stokes allowed him to remain at the school for a few days until he decided what he wanted to do and where he wanted to go. Van Gogh's prospects had never been so dismal or obscure. He tried to get a job as a missionary to the poor of London, which meant working in the most brutal slum areas, but he was turned down because he was too young.

Suddenly things took a brighter turn for van Gogh. He heard that Mr. Jones, a Methodist minister, needed an assistant, and when he inquired about the position, Mr. Jones offered it to him. He told van Gogh that he would be the permanent Bible teacher, instructing at Sunday school from the Bible, and added that he might even have a chance to preach in the church at Turnham Green.

Thinking he had found his opportunity at last, van Gogh was overjoyed. Half the night he lay awake reading the Bible, waiting for his chance to preach. Mr. Jones was slow to keep his promise, however. Also he could not pay him enough to live properly, and van Gogh often went without food. Still, he welcomed all the suffering he endured in the hopes of preaching in a church.

In the autumn his opportunity came; van Gogh preached his first sermon. It made very little impression. His halting, stammering speech and his accent were too difficult for the congregation to follow. His audience was restless, but he was in too much ecstasy to notice. He wrote his brother exultantly:

> Theo, your brother preached for the first time, last Sunday, in God's dwelling, of which is written, "In this place, I will give peace."
>
> When I was standing in the pulpit, I felt as if, emerging from a dark cave underground, I had come back to the friendly daylight, and it is a delightful thought that in the future wherever I shall be, I shall preach the Gospel; to do that well, one must have the Gospel in one's heart; may the Lord give it to me.

All the long treks on an empty stomach, the strain of many hours of Bible study, and the delivery of his

first sermon were too much for van Gogh. The young
man demanded more of his body than it could take,
but he would not give in. He preached a few more
times in different parts of London.

At last van Gogh became too ill and ceased to be of
value to Mr. Jones. Mostly because of his brother's
urging, van Gogh reluctantly decided that he would
return to his family once again. Mr. Jones, who was
very kind to the strange young man, expressed the
thought that his assistant was doing the right thing in
his present circumstances and bade him a warm good-
bye.

When van Gogh reached Etten for Christmas, looking very thin and haggard, his red hair ghastly against
the pallor of his skin, he was a dreadful sight. His
clothes were little better than rags, and he was sick
and exhausted. Because he had no money to spare, he
had walked miles, sleeping in parks or doorways
along the way home. Always having to fall back upon
his family, he loathed himself for his shortcomings.
Full of self-pity, tormented by the thought that he
was a complete failure, he believed he had been denied the greatest desire of his life—to serve God.

The family took in the returned prodigal once
more. Even their real concern, however, van Gogh
seemed to resent. In his heart he believed that se-
cretly they laughed at him, so he showed no gratitude
for their interest.

The problem of what to do with himself was not
solved until Uncle Vincent took matters in hand

again. "Do you think you would care to sell books?"
he asked his nephew. "I can arrange a position for you
in Dordrecht at Fussé and Braat, a very old and respected firm. They sell some paintings, but mostly
books. One of their biggest sellers is the Bible. I think
you might like working for them."

Wearily, van Gogh considered the offer. He had to
do something. Perhaps selling Bibles was a better way
to make a living than selling those dreadful pictures
at Goupil's. He agreed, to everyone's relief, to make
an effort.

Van Gogh explained his situation to his brother:

> There are many things that make it desirable,
> the being back in Holland near Father and Mother,
> and also near you and all the others. Then the
> salary would certainly be better than at Mr.
> Jones's, and it is one's duty to think of that, because
> later in life a man needs more.
>
> As to the religious work, I still do not give it up.
> Father is so broad-minded and so many-sided, and
> I hope in whatever circumstances I may be, some-
> thing of that will unfold in me.

Van Gogh had expressed to Mr. Jones the hope
that, when he was feeling better, he might be able to
return to England and work with him once more.
Now he admitted that this prospect was out of the
question. He wrote Mr. Jones, telling him he would
not be returning, and he asked his former employer to

think of him with charity. Mr. Jones was one employer with whom van Gogh always remained on good terms.

Feeling better, with new clothes on his back and good food in his stomach, van Gogh set out for Dordrecht, a small town between Etten and The Hague. And in January, 1877, he started work as a bookseller.

5 MISSION IN THE COAL MINES .

At Fussé and Braat van Gogh's employers soon discovered that he was almost useless to them, because he spent so much of his time sketching and reading the Bible. In addition, he was not a very pleasing clerk for such a dignified business. He glared at everyone, and already he had managed to make his new clothes shapeless and untidy.

Relations were very strained, but van Gogh did not seem to care. In fact, he seemed to take a savage delight in hurting himself. He went to churches more than ever now, and at mealtimes he prayed for a long time before touching his food. He tried to get his fellow boarders to attend church also and to think as he thought, but they grew afraid of his baleful glances and avoided him as much as possible. Why nobody loved him, he could not understand. He wanted to be good and kind and show others the right way to live, but somehow every effort turned to disaster. Van Gogh failed completely to realize what a big difference existed between his ideas and his behavior. He appealed to his brother for help in his present misery.

"I hate to see you so wretched, Vincent," Theo van Gogh replied. "Your religious desires are becoming morbid. Can't you understand that you should become a painter and take your talent for drawing seriously. Now, do send me more sketches!"

Van Gogh ignored the request. All Theo got in reply was more explanation of his brother's desire to preach. "I must think only of Jesus," he told him. "I will learn the Bible by heart. When this is done, my life will be changed."

One day van Gogh spoke to his employer, Braat, and told him he wished to become a preacher. Braat had nothing encouraging to say after the shock of van Gogh's bold statement. "I should like to see you leave us," he said. "But I seriously question your chance of ever becoming a minister."

Braat's disparaging tone and the hurtful truth he spoke made van Gogh fly into a rage. Faced with this kind of aggressiveness and all the other irritations he had suffered at the hands of this uncouth young man, Braat did not even try to hide his disgust. Scarcely more than three months after he had joined the firm, van Gogh was again without a job.

Reluctantly deciding to help his brother become a preacher, Theo van Gogh came to Dordrecht and talked for a long time with Vincent about his desires. Afterward Theo went to Amsterdam to consult with their family. All the relatives liked this quiet, gentle young man, who was so like his father and whose fine character and faith worked miracles for his brother. He convinced them that Vincent was sincere in his hopes to preach.

With the exception of Uncle Vincent, who disapproved altogether, the family agreed to do what they could to assist Vincent. One of his aunts was married to a famous preacher, a powerful man in the church, and they prevailed upon him to smooth the way for his wife's nephew. Accordingly, he arranged that van Gogh be accepted for two years of training for the ministry.

Although this scheme was not exactly as van Gogh would have had it, he looked forward to his new school. He wrote to his brother about it:

If I can only lose this depression that comes from knowing I have failed so often! If only the spirit of my father and grandfather may fall upon me. If only I may be given the strength to succeed in this. I do not want to hear any more reproaches like those so often hurled at me.

In May, 1877, twenty-four-year-old Vincent van Gogh set out for Amsterdam with high hopes, and for a year he worked hard at his studies. But soon he began to criticize the school. The examinations bothered him, and he had no tolerance for formal study. He was impatient to be out doing God's work.

After trying to reason with him, his teachers agreed he would never pass the examinations. Thus, after struggling for a whole year, van Gogh gave up. There was a terrible quarrel with his relatives in Amsterdam. Once more he had let the family down. Once more he had disgraced the good name of van Gogh.

The burden of failure was heavy as the young man set out again for his father's house in Etten. But in the back of his mind he knew the visit would be a short one. Van Gogh tried to explain his thoughts to his brother:

But sometimes a man says to himself: How shall I ever arrive! When I think of the past—when I think of the future of almost invincible difficulties, of much and difficult work, which I do not like, which I, or rather my evil self, would like to shirk; when I think of the eyes of so many fixed upon me—who will know where the fault is if I do not succeed, who will not make me trivial reproaches?

But as they are well tried and trained in everything that is right and virtuous, they will say, as it were by the expression of their faces: We have helped you and have been a light unto you; have you tried honestly?What is now our reward and the

fruit of our labor? See! When I think of all this, of
sorrow, of disappointment, of the fear of failure, of
disgrace—then I have the longing—I wish I were
far away from everything!

New thoughts, however, were being born in van
Gogh's mind. In Amsterdam he had heard stories
about a depressing, poverty-stricken coal-mining district in Belgium called Le Borinage. He decided to go
there, for the gloom of the place had a peculiar appeal for him. There he was needed. In Le Borinage,
among the lowest of the poor, he would spread the
word and would bring the light of God to the suffering miners. They would not despise him as others
had. They would welcome him, and he would become
one of them.

First van Gogh contacted his old former employer,
Mr. Jones, in England. Would Mr. Jones help him get
placed as a missionary? He was twenty-five years old
now, and nobody could say he was too young.

Mr. Jones cared enough to try to help, and he made
the journey to Etten to discuss the matter with van
Gogh and his parents. "But," he warned, "you must
have several months' training first. Then you will be
sent out as a lay preacher. There is a school where I
have connections in Brussels, and I will introduce you
there. If you work hard, you can probably rise to a
better position in missionary work."

Van Gogh's heart sank at the prospect of more
training. But as there was no other way he agreed,

and with his father and Mr. Jones he went to Brussels to inspect the school and settle details. This school at Laeken was run for the purpose of training evangelical ministers.

When he returned home, a feeling of great peacefulness settled over van Gogh. He was like a different person. There were no arguments in the house. He expressed his optimism in a letter to his younger brother:

It does one good to feel that one has still a brother, who lives and walks on this earth; when one has many things to think of, and many things to do, one sometimes gets the feeling: Where am I? What am I doing? Where am I going?—and one's brain reels, but then such a well-known voice as yours, or rather a well-known handwriting, makes one feel again firm ground under one's feet.

Van Gogh barely tolerated the training at the missionary school, considering it of no value for the work he would be doing. Once more he began to criticize and question the school curriculum. Rapidly exasperating all the teachers, he disputed everything he was taught, and he refused to sit at a desk, preferring to write on his knees. Van Gogh finally grew so aggressive that he antagonized everybody. When, in three months, the time came to consider his nomination, he was refused. Oddly enough, he did not seem to mind.

The school principal sent for his father. Pastor van Gogh had been shocked by his son many times, but he was hardly prepared for the way he found him in Brussels. Van Gogh had not been sleeping or eating well, and he looked like a scarecrow. In desperation, the pastor appealed to the principal to let his son serve as a missionary in Le Borinage without salary. The principal agreed, urging van Gogh to continue with his studies.

Van Gogh wrote to his brother about what had been happening, hoping that he would understand his decision to go to Le Borinage.

Now there is in the south of Belgium, in the neighborhood of Mons, up to the French frontiers, a district called the Borinage, that has a peculiar population of laborers who work in the numerous coal mines. I should very much like to go there as an evangelist, preaching the Gospel to the poor— that means those who need it most, and for whom it is so well suited—and during the week devoting myself to teaching.

If I could work quietly for about three years in such a district, always learning and observing, then I should not come back from there without having something to say that was really worth hearing. I say so in all humility and yet with confidence. I should be ready about my thirtieth year, able to begin with a peculiar training and experience, able to master my work better, and riper for it than now.

In December, 1878, van Gogh left for a village called Pâturages, near the town of Mons, in Le Borinage. His father would allow him what few francs he could spare each month. When he arrived at Pâturages, neat and clean, he found lodgings with a peddler named Van der Haegen.

In Le Borinage—indeed a depressing place—clouds of dirty brown smoke hung in the air. The men and women who mined the coal were mercilessly exploited, and their life was hard and short. There was a good deal of sickness due to gas fumes and coal dust. But van Gogh felt at home in this awful place. The miners' speech was crude, like his, and they, too, had little to be joyful about.

Word soon spread that this stranger was a missionary. Van Gogh started his work by visiting the sick and helping wherever he could. He preached in stables, halls, sheds, anywhere a group could gather. For a while he was happy and found a kind of contentment in what he was doing.

Reports on his work were very good, and in January, 1879, he was finally salaried on a six-months' trial basis. His superiors sent him to work in the village of Wasmes, with orders to visit the sick, to give Bible instruction, and to teach the children.

Now that he had what he so badly wanted, van

Gogh felt a surge of triumph. His struggles were over.
These people recognized him as a working servant of
God, and they accepted him as one of them. So he
believed.

Van Gogh moved into a hut meaner than that of
the poorest miner. He gave away everything he had—
his money, his bed, his good clothes. In place of them
he wore leggings, which he had cut out from coal
sacks, and an old, discarded soldier's jacket. All his
clean linens he gave to the sick and the poor. To make
himself as much like the Borains as possible, he even
smeared his face with coal dust. Only when he had
given up all luxuries, which set him apart from his
people, did he feel that he was one of them in truth.

In his letters van Gogh shared his thoughts with his
brother constantly. He wrote:

In these dark days here, snow has fallen. Everything reminds me of the paintings of Brueghel.
What we see here also makes me think of the work
of Albrecht Dürer. There are paths here full of
brambles and twisted old trees with queer roots
which are exactly like that road in Dürer's engrav-
ing, *The Knight, Death and the Devil.*

Van Gogh also described some of his adventures
to his brother:

I went on a particularly interesting expedition,
six hours down into a mine. It is one of the oldest

and most dangerous in the district. It is a gloomy place, and at first sight the whole surroundings have a mournful and dreary look. The workers are emaciated and pale with fever. They are tired and worn out, old for their age. Round the mine stand the wretched hovels of the miners with a few dead trees blackened with smoke, hedges full of brambles, heaps of ashes and manure, mountains of worthless coal.

Imagine a row of cells in a rather narrow and low passage supported by rough timber. In each of these cells a miner, in a coarse linen suit, filthy and black, is busy cutting coal by the pale light of a small lamp. In some of those cells the miner stands erect; in others he lies on the ground. Some of the miners work in the *maintenages* (maintenance area); others load the cut coal in small carts; this is done especially by children, boys as well as girls. There is also a stable yard down there, seven meters underground, with about seven old horses.

Van Gogh tried to conduct his mission by living according to the teachings of Jesus as he interpreted them. Alas, what Jesus taught was one thing; what men did was something else again. Van Gogh's Christlike gestures were completely misunderstood, and people thought he was very strange indeed. They ignored his honest and valuable efforts in caring for the sick and considered his visits down into the mines, sharing the dangers of the workers, stupid. He must be mad! They had to enter the mines. But he did not.

The gossip spread about this odd preacher who had come among the villagers. Word got back to his superiors about his behavior, and an inspector was sent to check the rumors. When he made his report, van Gogh was ordered to dress properly and behave like a correct missionary or leave. Pastor van Gogh was also notified.

The pastor made the journey to Wasmes to see for himself the dirty skeleton his son had become. Eventually he managed to persuade him to move back to his lodgings with the peddler and to wear clean clothes again. Then with a heavy heart he returned to his parsonage.

For a short while things were peaceful. There were no more complaints from his superiors. Van Gogh shifted the emphasis of his work to the sick, aiding them with a skill and tenderness few would have believed him capable of. If he visited an ill person and a bandage was needed, he thought nothing of tearing strips off his shirt. This kind of Christianity, he felt, was the most practical. In his own way, he was reacting to the rebelliousness that was beginning to grow among the miners.

Van Gogh really loved the Borains and worked hard in their behalf. He was sickened to see them so badly exploited and treated like animals, and he began to question. For a change his questioning was healthy. How could he preach of a better life in heaven to such poor downtrodden souls? Were they not justified in asking why life was so difficult on earth? The answers he found disturbed him. In the summer his anger reached a boiling point.

There was a terrible explosion at the mine, and in the rescue efforts van Gogh worked on the injured like a man possessed. His hatred of injustice kept him going without food or care for himself. When the miners, following this calamity, went on strike for better conditions, van Gogh joined their leaders, urging them on. The church council warned him that his only job was to care for the spiritual welfare of these people and that he should leave their political battles alone. But van Gogh, sure of the justice of his stand, ignored the council. In July he was given three months to find another position.

He shrugged off the three months' notice. He had not a penny in his pockets, but with a bundle of his pitiful belongings and a roll of sketches under his arm, he strode purposefully toward Brussels, many miles distant. There he would see Pastor Pietersen, a man Mr. Jones had introduced him to long ago. The pastor was also an amateur artist and had talked about art and religion previously with him. Now van Gogh intended to call upon him for advice.

On his journey he again slept in fields, doorways— in fact, wherever he could lie down. From time to time, he managed to sell a few drawings or exchange them for a meal.

Van Gogh was a dreadful apparition when he arrived at the pastor's house. His daughter, who opened the door, was so frightened by the sight of him that she fled screaming for her father. With difficulty Pastor Pietersen finally recognized van Gogh. He fed him, cleaned him, and, most importantly, was able to calm the nervous, troubled young man.

Reporting on their son's visit, Pastor Pietersen wrote to his parents. "The trouble is," he told them, "that he stands in his own way. He has no clear idea of what he wants or of how to set about finding out. He seems sure of only one thing; he loves the people of Le Borinage and considers them his own."

A new notion, however, was crystallizing in van Gogh's mind. Conversations with the pastor about art started him thinking that he had neglected his drawing for too long.

To his brother he wrote: "It was in the depths of this misery that I felt my energy return and that I said to myself, whatever happens, I shall make good. I shall take up my pencil which I abandoned, and I shall start drawing again." Still the thought did not really penetrate his mind that Theo had been urging him to take his drawing seriously for several years.

When Vincent showed the pastor his drawings, the pastor bought a few of them in order to give him funds without embarrassing him. In doing so, he may have served the world far better than he knew.

Feeling strong, with food in his stomach and a little money in his pocket, van Gogh decided to return to Le Borinage. There he spent much of his time sketch-

POTATO EATERS

Nuenen, 1885   Collection V. W. van Gogh, Laren

ing. Soon after his arrival, he received a letter from his parents. "Come home," they begged, "even if only for a little while. The rest will do you good and a change of scene will be beneficial, we are sure." Sick and weary, van Gogh agreed to go to Etten for a visit in August, although he was skeptical of their concern for him.

When his parents saw the state he had come to, they upbraided him for bringing such disgrace upon the family. The sorry condition of their son would be the talk of Etten. Suffering severely from a sense of hopeless failure, van Gogh endured their reproaches, but again he retreated behind a wall of silence, speaking to no one unless he was spoken to. Thus, the visit was a miserable time for the whole family. Van Gogh left as soon as he could and returned to his miners.

Eventually he was forced to realize that, for all his desire, he was not really one of these people. The elders of their church had forbidden him to preach to them, but even the wish to do so had left him. Van Gogh went from day to day, sketching purposelessly. He eked out a precarious living on the few francs he got from home. Most of the time he was hungry. His brother visited him once, hoping to lift him from the lethargy he had settled into. Although they did not really quarrel, Theo felt that his brother was unnecessarily cruel to his parents and said so.

As a result of the harsh words, for nine months no letters passed between the two brothers who loved each other so much.

6 THE DECISION

In August, 1880, unable to bear his complete isolation any longer, van Gogh, now twenty-seven years old, broke the dreadful silence between him and his brother with a long letter.

> You have become a stranger to me up to a certain point, and I am also more of a stranger to you than you think. Can we not come together once more? I think my decision not to remain at Etten was a wise one. I have become more or less unmanageable and suspect in the eyes of my family. Whatever I do, I do not inspire confidence. How then could I be useful in any way to any one? I am therefore convinced that it is to my own interest and to that of everyone else for me to go away and to remain

away. I am very easily swayed by passions. I am capable of doing—indeed I am likely to do—things which are more or less mad and which I am usually somewhat sorry for afterwards.

Now, bearing this in mind, what am I to do? Ought I to consider myself a dangerous fellow, incapable of doing anything worthwhile? I do not think so. My job is to put my own passions to some good use.

In this letter, at least, van Gogh showed an awareness of his own unruly temperament. His astonishing appeal to his brother for help went on:

I should be quite pleased if you could see me otherwise than merely as a ne'er-do-well, for there are many kinds of ne'er-do-wells. There is the man who is a ne'er-do-well from laziness and meanness of character, from the baseness of his nature; you can take me for one of those if you like. Then there is the other ne'er-do-well, who is so in spite of himself, who is inwardly tortured by a desire for action, who does nothing because it is impossible for him to do anything, because it is as if he were imprisoned within something.

I am good for something. I feel that there is a reason for my existence. I know that I could be quite a different kind of man. What then could I be useful for, what purpose could I serve? There is something inside me—what can it be? This is quite another kind of ne'er-do-well; you can take me for one of these if you like.

Men are often incapable of doing anything, for they are prisoners in a horrible kind of cage. Do you know what makes the prison disappear? Any deep and serious affection. If we are friends, if we are brothers, if we love, we can magically open the prison doors.

When sympathy returns, life is born again. If it were possible for you to see anything else in me than a ne'er-do-well of the wrong kind, I should be very pleased.

Contact with his brother again established, van Gogh, with childlike simplicity, quietly accepted the call of his genius. Perhaps in studying art he would find his salvation. In any case, he had to find something to give his existence meaning, and he could see no other prospects anywhere. If he developed his natural skill, he would be fulfilling his desire to serve God and mankind.

In painting, he realized, one expresses an unselfish kind of love. Artists, putting their awareness of life and people onto canvas, capture moments of truth for all time, and yet they, as creators, remain unseen. After much thought van Gogh came to a valuable conclusion. Great artists had not said everything there was to say about life after all; *he* would fill the gap!

The appalling living conditions in Le Borinage of the miners and of the weavers, hunched over their looms in their tiny, poorly lit cottages, had been overlooked by other artists. Although van Gogh did not know how to paint yet, he could draw them, and, in this way, serve them best. In his new role, he would praise God and draw attention to the plight of these unhappy people. Van Gogh had been reading Charles Dickens's stories of hardship among the poor and forgotten. The tales had made a big impression on him and had helped him shape the idea to which he now devoted himself.

At last, he had found a satisfying medium in which to express himself. Although his character and confused values remained the same, a profound change came over him. Van Gogh began to work at his sketching as if demons were pursing him, fearful that his subjects would escape him before he could capture them with his pencil. Drawing after drawing flowed from his skilled hands. He worked far into the night, in feeble light, forgetting even to eat. He wrote to his brother and to his old employer at The Hague asking for books on art. In an effort to learn, he copied the works of all the artists he believed great.

Theo van Gogh tried to persuade his brother to move to Paris. He felt sure that he would make more rapid progress there. "You will mingle with other painters, grow with them, learn from them, and thus make your way more quickly," he urged.

Van Gogh, however, was afraid to go. He had been rejected and mocked too often. "I might lose my soul in the elegant Paris studios of those successful paint-

ers who dominate Paris art," he explained. Nevertheless, his present situation was becoming intolerable.
The people where he lodged were as kind as their
limits allowed. A corner of the room had been cleared
for him, but he was an untidy worker and it rapidly
became crowded with his materials. Night after
night, day after day, he sat hunched over paper,
drawing in the poor lamplight. When the weather
permitted he worked outside. The money his brother
sent him was all he had to live on, and he took it for
granted. "Perhaps," he told his brother, "when I have
perfected my techniques, I will come to Paris."

In October, without a word to anyone, van Gogh
left, not for Paris as Theo had hoped, but for Brussels.
He found a small room and settled in it, living on
bread, potatoes, and coffee. When his brother heard
of the change, he immediately sent him introductions
to people he knew there. One of Theo's friends advised van Gogh to enter the Academy in Brussels. He
tried and failed. He went to the home of a young
artist, named Alexander van Rappard, his brother had
spoken of. When van Rappard answered the knock at
his studio door, undoubtedly he was astounded by the
bag of bones standing on his threshold. But good
manners and his strong friendship for the gentle and
aristocratic Theo made him invite van Gogh inside.

Through this connection van Gogh was brought
into the circle of artists in Brussels, and he began to
learn a great deal. He moved into van Rappard's

studio to work, immediately making a shambles of it. Van Rappard tolerated van Gogh's black moods of despair when he failed to get his drawing in the right proportion and perspective. He even helped him find models from whom he could make life studies.

Despite their skepticism, van Gogh's parents and relatives, hoping he had finally settled down to work, encouraged him whenever they could. There was nothing else they could do.

As usual, van Gogh quarreled with his new friends before long. Again they were all wrong; he was right. In his newfound enthusiasm, he dreamed of a colony of painters working side by side, sharing their money and helping to develop each other's talents. Their purpose would be to enrich and enlighten the world. He did not take kindly to the criticism, "Perhaps first you should learn to show a little appreciation and concern for those who support you and help you make your way."

Models were hard to locate, for van Gogh seldom could pay them. His offensiveness to those artists in Brussels who had befriended him and his high living costs made it necessary for him to search elsewhere. Theo van Gogh again urged him to come to Paris. Again he refused. He decided to return home. At Etten he could find plenty of peasant models.

Theo van Gogh smoothed the way, as always, for his brother. Vincent promised him that he would improve his appearance and not disgrace their family by walking about like a tramp. His parents, in turn, vowed that they would try to be patient and avoid antagonizing their troublesome oldest son.

By April, 1881, van Gogh was at his parents' home. Shortly after his arrival Theo came for a visit. The pastor and his wife trusted their younger son's judgment and, despite their fears, began to believe he was right when he said that Vincent had found himself at last. Van Gogh really was on his best behavior, and for a while there was harmony. But sometimes, it seemed to him, his parents overemphasized the prodigal son attitude. And he grew restless.

As the weeks passed van Gogh became an increasingly difficult trial. He seemed to attach no importance to tidiness or cleanliness. Even though his parents had given him fresh clothes, they soon looked as bad as the rags that they had thrown out. The weather was good, and he often went out to the village and fields for hours on end. His father feared he was making a bad impression on his parishioners.

Van Rappard came to Etten for a short time. While he was there, van Gogh could not have been more pleasant, and his parents' hopes for him rose again. If he could have such a gentle and refined friend, one who would come so far to visit him, perhaps Theo was right, and he was not so bad after all. From now on things would be better. Even Uncle Vincent, seeing his nephew apparently had found the kind of work he wanted, was a little forgiving.

Bubbling with enthusiasm van Gogh kept his brother informed of his progress.

I drew a peasant with a spade, many times, digging in different positions. I drew a sower and a girl with a broom twice. Then I drew a woman with a white bonnet, peeling potatoes. I drew a shepherd leaning on his staff. Another drawing is of an old peasant who is ill. He is sitting on a chair by the fireplace with his head on his hands, his elbows resting on his knees. I am beginning to work with a brush; sometimes I use Chinese ink, and occasionally I try a little color.

Despite his new happiness the desire for a love of his own still haunted him. Sometimes the gravestone of his dead brother appeared in a nightmare, and he feared the recurrence of these bad dreams. Unwittingly, his parents were the cause of yet another blow that fell upon the luckless artist.

Pastor van Gogh and his wife were concerned about a young cousin who recently had been widowed and left with a child. They asked her to stay with them for a while.

Van Gogh had known Kee Vos slightly when he was studying in Amsterdam for the ministry. Her husband had been alive then, so he had not visited her often or paid any special attention to her. When Kee arrived at the parsonage in Etten, he found her completely charming. He liked her small son even more, and soon he and the boy became inseparable. The pastor and his wife were astonished at their son's consideration and thoughtfulness. They had never seen this side of him before.

Kee did not like Vincent van Gogh when she knew him in Amsterdam, and she did not like him now in Etten. However, there could be no denying that her son adored this strange man. Gradually, Kee's attitude toward him softened. She spoke kindly to him, and she learned to look at him without feeling repulsed by his appearance. Soon Kee began to accompany van Gogh when he took her boy for walks.

Because of van Gogh's gentleness with the child, his parents were deceived into thinking that he had found himself at last. But he had not changed. He was convinced that marrying Kee was the answer to his problems. With her as his wife, his blossoming artistic talent would soar to the heights. The more he saw of Kee, the more he thought about her, and the more determined he became that she would be his. Cruelly, he broke the idyll of peace at the parsonage.

Finding Kee alone one day, van Gogh abruptly poured out his love for her. Looking at him with distaste she said, "Don't ever speak to me of this again. Never, no never!" After she told his parents what had happened, Kee quickly went with her son back to Amsterdam.

Van Gogh bombarded Kee with letters, which she did not answer. He poured out his frustration in a letter to his brother. "My God, how terrible it was when she said, 'Never, no never!' Well, I am not resigned. It must be she and no one else!"

Pastor van Gogh's toleration of his son's ravings came swiftly to an end. The terrible arguments were making his wife ill. "It is best that you leave this house, Vincent," he said. "There is nothing more we can do or say. Your dreadful behavior is too much of a torment to your mother."

Attempting to justify himself once more, van Gogh wrote to his brother about the situation.

I should like it very much if you could persuade Father and Mother to less pessimism and to more good courage and humanity. I have been complaining a little about Father and Mother, but, after all, except that they do not understand the least bit about it all and could only call what I did this summer 'untimely and indelicate' (till I requested them quite firmly not to use such expressions any more), they are good to me and kinder than ever. But I should rather they could understand more of my thoughts and opinions about many things.

Theirs is a system of resignation to which I cannot resign myself. One word from Mother this summer would have given me the opportunity of saying things to *her* which could not be said in public. But Mother very decidedly refused to say that word; on the contrary, she cut off every opportunity for me.

The quiet determination of his father shocked van Gogh into a more rational attitude. He wrote to Theo to intervene and stop this ultimatum. After all, he had nowhere else to go. He reminded his brother of the great progress he was making. To interrupt his work now would be harmful.

Then he ceased arguing with his parents and fell into a grim silence. Theo van Gogh wrote, begging his parents to reconsider and let Vincent stay at the parsonage. Since he was at least quiet again, his father did not insist that he leave.

Still, no answers to his letters came from Amsterdam. Van Gogh grew frantic. He could not accept the fact that Kee did not want him. Somehow he would make her understand the profundity of his love.

In one last effort to bend her to his will, van Gogh left suddenly for Amsterdam. When he arrived at Kee's house, the family was about to sit down for dinner, but Kee was nowhere in sight. Her relatives were cordial to him and invited him to eat with them. He learned that Kee had indeed been there and had left the house immediately when she learned that van Gogh was calling.

When the family asked him if he would stay the night, he refused curtly. Before he left, he was told— politely, but in a way that could not be misunderstood—that his attentions to Kee were unwanted. He was to cease trying to see her and to stop writing letters, which she burned without bothering to read.

Van Gogh refused to accept this rejection. Next

day he returned to the house. Still, Kee would not see him. He left, only to return again in the evening. He was told once more that his persistence was not appreciated. Then he committed a horrifying act. Standing on a table near to him was a burning oil lamp. Blind with rage, frustration, and misery van Gogh plunged his hand into the flame and held it there. "Let me see her for as long as I can hold my hand in this flame," he pleaded. Quickly, someone ran and put out the lamp. "No," they told him, "you will *not* see her!"

For the first time, the violence in van Gogh's nature had been expressed physically. Staggered by their determination, he stumbled from the house and fell into a black depression. Aimlessly he wandered, not knowing where to go or what to do. His dream of Kee was shattered.

After drifting for a while, van Gogh went to The Hague and made peace with his relatives there. He thanked them profusely for the books they had sent him, and, this time, he generally made a favorable impression. They now accepted the fact that he was sincere and serious about his work.

His cousin Jet, Aunt Sophie's daughter, had married Anton Mauve, the painter van Gogh had long admired. Somewhat timidly, he asked if he might stay with them for a few weeks.

When van Gogh showed Mauve his sketches of the Brabant peasants, he praised them highly. Mauve asked him to show what he could do with a still life he had arranged of a cabbage, potatoes, a pair of wooden clogs, and a drape, and van Gogh was delighted when Mauve suggested that he try working with charcoal and chalk, watercolors and oils, in addition to pencil.

Until Mauve took him seriously, van Gogh had not been conscious of his deep love of color, even though he was graphic about it in his letters. Now under Mauve's influence, color began gradually to appear in his work. Never had van Gogh felt such excitement as when he watched Mauve apply colors to canvas. Eagerly, almost frantically, he experimented with oils and watercolors himself in a feverish effort to learn how to use these new materials. Despite van Gogh's extremes, Mauve and his wife respected his desperate desire to learn, and they were patient and kindly to their country relative. All too soon, however, the struggling artist ran out of money with which to buy painting supplies, and he could not borrow more from Mauve and his friends.

His father was angry when van Gogh wrote for more money. What had he done with all he had been given? How could he spend it so fast? Pastor van Gogh complained to Theo and other members of the family.

Learning of his father's criticism of him, van Gogh was furious and explained the situation to his brother. "Anton Mauve believes I will be a saleable artist very soon if I can continue this progress," he wrote. "This is high praise and encouragement from such a master."

Receiving Mauve's praise and encouragement meant everything to him. He needed the attention desperately. Van Gogh's plea, however, made little impression, for no money was available. There was nothing to do but go home to Etten. Inevitably, trouble followed his return.

7 HIS OWN

■

On Christmas day, 1881, van Gogh refused to accompany his parents to church. The pastor was forced to tell him once again to leave his house. He offered his son money to see him on his way, but, full of bluster and false pride, van Gogh would not accept it. "I want none of your charity," he shouted, forgetting how many times in the past it had saved his life.

Van Gogh went directly to The Hague and told his sad tale to Anton Mauve, who listened sympathetically. He and his wife loaned him some money for furniture and helped him find a room of his own. To please them, van Gogh bought himself a decent suit of clothes.

When he had settled down, van Gogh wrote to his brother and told him all Mauve had done. Also, he wanted to know, was Theo going to help him? When his letter was not answered, van Gogh grew worried.

Finally, he did hear from him. Very angry over Vincent's recent behavior at Etten, Theo wrote: "Why do you give our parents so much trouble? They do not deserve it. Besides, they're getting older now, and Father is unable to understand your bitterness. They have done the best they could for you. Such heartless behavior I do not and will not condone!" Nevertheless, his brother also sent some money.

Van Gogh was relieved to have the money and tried to gloss over the references to the troubles at home. Now he could go on working, and Anton Mauve was making him work hard. He had no remorse for his attitude toward his parents; his struggle for independence of spirit blinded him. "After all," he told his brother, "isn't my father forever telling me 'You'll be the death of me'? It's just a trick to get me to conform. I cannot do it, Theo. I cannot. I must go my own way."

At first, Anton Mauve and his wife saw only the best side of van Gogh. They were impressed by his eagerness and his ability to learn. His violent reactions to things seemed to them merely a childlike naïveté.

For a while all went smoothly. Mauve helped van Gogh enormously with his studies. He let him use his studio, and he gave him plaster hands and feet and busts to draw. Van Gogh willingly accepted Mauve's criticism of his efforts and advice. "You should first make watercolor sketches, Vincent," he explained. "They will sell more quickly. If an artist is to be independent, if he is to do the kind of work he knows he must, he must first sell work that will bring the means of his independence." Van Gogh struggled hard to master watercolors and oils, and Mauve was always there, urging him on.

He was happy and enjoyed the circle of artists in which he now moved. When van Gogh returned to his own room at night, however, he was very lonely. The warmth of the relationship between Mauve and his wife he witnessed daily. Thoughts of Kee still haunted him. He wanted a wife of his own, someone who would love him as he was.

Van Gogh solved his problem—or thought he had —in his usual brash, forceful way. He met a woman named Christine. She was an unkempt, unwholesome person, a wanderer who drifted around with her mother, living each day as it came. To van Gogh, however, she was magnificent. Disregarding all consequences, he promptly decided he was madly in love with her. She was the rock upon which he would build his future! He called her Sien, meaning *his own*. In his twisted mind, Sien was a poor unfortunate creature. He decided he would be her champion. He would make her his wife and take care of her and her mother. Although his brother was his sole means of support, van Gogh thought nothing of adding to his burden.

Sien fell sick, and when she came out of the hospital van Gogh took her and her mother back to his small room. He had worked hard on the tiny place, and despite its limitations had made it snug.

Van Gogh wrote an explanation in a letter to Theo.

I took her as a model. Thanks to God's help, I was able to save her from hunger and cold by sharing my own bread with her. The woman is attached to me now, like a tame dove. As for me, I can only marry once, and how can I do better than to marry her? It is the only way in which I can continue to help her.

Theo was very upset by the news of this attachment. Surely his brother had better sense. Anton Mauve, van Gogh's relatives—everybody who knew the artist, in fact—were outraged by his latest behavior. Yet van Gogh convinced himself that he was very happy. He had all a man could ask for—a home and a good woman in it who would soon be his wife. Totally unaware of the truth, he believed Sien loved him for himself alone. Van Gogh made several studies and the best one of Sien he called *Sorrow*. Soon, he told himself, he would be selling more than an occasional sketch.

At this time a new interest absorbed van Gogh, so he was not aware of the scandal that was spreading about him. The young artist Breitner had befriended

him, and together they went regularly to soup kitch-
ens and haunts of the poor, spending the days sketching and painting the people. As always, van Gogh—
while protesting how much he loved such people—
easily forgot their sensitivities. Entirely obsessed by
his own need to draw them, he boldly placed himself
before his subjects and spoke to them roughly, sometimes asking them to rearrange their clothing for a
certain effect. Van Gogh was totally unaware that he
appeared to be ordering them to sit for him.

Even paupers have pride. The people began to
resent him and complained bitterly whenever he
showed up with Breitner. "Mr. van Gogh," a man told
him one day, "we cannot have you upsetting these
poor souls we are trying to help. You are causing too
much uneasiness among them. Please do not come
here again. If you do, we cannot be responsible for
what might happen."

Van Gogh was astounded. He had not the slightest
idea he had been making himself a nuisance. Unhap-
pily, he had to give up his source of free models.
Despite the discord, Breitner liked van Gogh, and he
continued to work beside him, although not quite so
often as before.

Soon van Gogh discovered that the strain of supporting himself, Sien, and her mother was more than
he had bargained on. His brother could not spare
more money than he was sending now. "After all," he
reminded Vincent, "I have to keep myself, too. I must
maintain a certain standard of living for the sake of

my work. There are many important and wealthy people with whom I do business, and I must be sociable."

Van Gogh and Sien began to quarrel and irritate each other. Sien put him off when he mentioned marriage. She began to dislike the attention from him and the stares and whispers directed at her on the streets. She began to yearn for her own free and easy way of life.

In addition, van Gogh became aware of the murmurings of the scandal surrounding him. He fought back the only way he knew. Those who criticized him he criticized twice as bitterly. He even quarreled with Mauve, smashing to the floor a plaster cast he had been loaned, and Mauve told him to stay away from his studio. And so the latest idol fell.

To make matters worse, van Gogh argued with an art dealer who had been encouraging him. He refused to change the kind of subject he was painting. After telling van Gogh, "You are not an artist; you have started too late," the man told him never again to show his face in the gallery.

Van Gogh grew bitter about Mauve and his friends. "I do not need any of them," he cried. "I will go my own way. Painters they call themselves! They paint but the shadows of life. I will get the very stuff of life onto my own canvases!"

Lack of proper food, constant emotional outbursts, and the burden of his financial difficulties once again plagued van Gogh. "Please do your utmost to come soon, brother," he wrote to Theo van Gogh in an appeal for money. "I do not know how long I can hold out! I either had to fast, or work less, and as far as possible I chose the first alternative—until the time came when I was too weak."

Theo van Gogh urged his brother to restore himself to the good graces of the art dealer if possible. He also told him to make up with his artist friends. "Get rid of Sien," Theo advised. "She is the chief cause of your grief. As for me, I send you all the money I can spare. I live as frugally as possible in order to help you. I believe in you Vincent, with all my heart. But you must put your own house in order."

Van Gogh did make an effort to renew his friendships. He called on Anton Mauve and asked him to criticize some of his work. Mauve coldly rebuffed him, telling van Gogh that their relationship was ended for all time and that he considered him a vicious person.

When the furore about his son's activities reached Pastor van Gogh's ears, he went to see for himself, and he pleaded with Vincent to change his ways. All he got for his trouble was a show of terrible temper. "They are jealous of my home and family and my work!" van Gogh yelled at his father almost hysterically. "I am better than all of them." Seeing the hopelessness of his task, the pastor sadly gave up and went home.

Theo van Gogh also visited Vincent, to see what he might do about the situation. Unable to combat his brother's stubbornness, he decided to tolerate the situation, and he gave van Gogh sufficient funds to last about a year.

Van Gogh seemed truly grateful, and he wrote to Theo:

Dear Brother, I am still quite under the impression of your visit. I had really often suppressed the desire to paint; through what you gave me, a new horizon has been opened to me; I think I am privileged above thousands of others because you have removed so many barriers for me. Many a painter cannot go on because of the expense, and I cannot express to you in words how thankful I am. I began later than others, and to make up for that lost time I must work doubly hard; in spite of my ardor, I should have to stop if it were not for you. I think it is a delightful prospect to be able to work a whole year without anxiety.

Sien herself solved part of the problem. She simply walked out of van Gogh's room with her mother and refused to go back. Once more the unhappy man had lost everything, and bitter thoughts began to torment him. He suffered from nightmares and severe headaches. In his misery, he finally saw Sien as she really was, and the knowledge hurt him deeply. He could not hold even such a lowly creature as she! He had been rejected by a woman of the streets!

In a rare moment of common sense van Gogh remembered that his old acquaintance, van Rappard, had talked of the beauty of Drenthe. One could live cheaply in this old town in northern Holland. Also, the peasants in the area might be used as models. Hoping he could persuade van Rappard to join him there, he set out for Drenthe.

The countryside, he found, was an endless stretch of moorland and bogs. To him it was a beautiful wonderland. He told his brother about it in one of his letters:

Imagine the banks of a canal stretching for miles and miles as in a landscape. Flat strips of country, of different colors, become narrower and narrower as they reach the horizon. Here and there they are accentuated by huts built of turf or little farms, or a few thin birches and poplars; oaks, heaps of peat are everywhere, and there is a constant stream of barges laden with peat from the bogs. Here and there, I saw some lean cows of exquisite coloring. Everything here is perfect and beautiful, and I love it.

The peasants of Drenthe found the red-haired painter in their midst very odd. It was December and most of them refused to pose for him outside. Only one or two posed in his room for a fee, and they felt uncomfortable in his presence. Also, van Gogh had little money to spare.

As the dark days of winter approached, van Gogh

himself took on their gloom. He was feeling frustrated. His timing had been bad. He had chosen to go out into the open country when other artists were beginning to do a winter's work in their studios. Feeling forlorn and lost, he made his way back to The Hague. With nowhere else to turn van Gogh went home. His parents had now moved to another small town called Nuenen.

In Nuenen, the gossip soon spread. People could scarcely believe that this horrible-looking creature could be their gentle pastor's son. He had never mentioned such a son to them.

Van Gogh had been home scarcely a few days before he became savage. His parents did not utter a word of reproach this time, but fed him and did all they could for his comfort. Perhaps van Gogh's conscience at this forgiveness hurt him. With his sense of failure burdening him, the ministrations of his parents undoubtedly only angered him more.

Van Gogh fell into a complete silence. When he wanted something, he scribbled notes demanding it. He was rude to visitors, holding out a single finger in greeting. He insisted that his family serve as models and that he be allowed freedom to paint whenever he chose. Van Gogh ate wherever he happened to be, painting furiously between mouthfuls of food. Leaving paints and brushes everywhere, he turned the well-ordered house upside down.

After a while van Gogh decided to move into the old parsonage washhouse. His family made it warm and comfortable for him and even put in a bigger window so he could have more light. He shut himself up alone—day after day—to sketch and paint.

He knew people were gossiping about him every time he bothered to stroll into the village. Let them talk! The more fun they made of him, the more defiant he became. He ceased to care for anything except to play the person they thought he was. His clothes were so worn they were nearly falling off his back. One day he left the house and made a purchase, which he said he chose because it was so cheap.

A stranger sight had never been seen on the streets of Nuenen than when van Gogh strolled about in his new tweed suit. Its color was a lilac shade, and it was mottled with orange and yellow spots.

8 MARGOT

■

Vincent van Gogh was a bewildering paradox. Although he could not recognize the trait in himself, he was capable of self-deceit, and he went to great lengths to justify his acts to others. For the most part, van Gogh found scant fault with himself, though he raved over his parents' lack of understanding and their constant bickering about the way he dressed and the way he lived. He seldom reaped anything but confusion, sorrow, and pain. His sufferings, mental and physical, would have broken a weaker man long before, but there was an animal strength in him that enabled him to suffer these misfortunes and keep going.

Somehow his brother continued to smooth the way between van Gogh and those he so frequently antagonized. Despite his faith in his brother's talent, however, even Theo became exasperated. He reminded Vincent that, "Far from my being to blame for Sien's leaving you, it was your own fault for getting involved with her. She didn't care the tiniest bit about you."

As unpredictable as ever, in January, 1884, van Gogh revealed a side of his nature that was seldom in much evidence. His mother had been on a visit to friends, and on her return she slipped from a train carriage and broke her hip. In those days modern drugs and pain killers were unknown, and she was in great pain. There was despair and confusion at the parsonage when she was brought home. She was not expected to live, and if she did, she would spend a minimum of six months as a bedridden invalid. Pastor van Gogh could not bear to see his wife suffer, yet he was helpless in the face of disaster. The girls only got in the way when they were home, and young brother Cor was still a schoolboy. So the major burden of caring for his mother fell upon van Gogh. With a sureness he seldom showed outside his painting, this oldest son took control of the family in its time of trouble. And he reveled in his burden. Van Gogh brushed aside the praise he received, but in his heart a very great satisfaction warmed him. Now he, the ugly, weak character, was strong. He held the family together and gave them support when they needed it most. And for a while, he found peace and rest. He could even sleep well, without being troubled by unpleasant dreams or nightmares.

Van Gogh had learned a lot from his experiences in Le Borinage. His knowledge gained from the mine disaster and from his attention to the injured in those grim days was very useful now. All kindness and sympathy, he changed his mother's position when her bed became uncomfortable and did everything he possibly could for her. He spoke gently to everyone. And so good a nurse was he that his mother was able to be up and about in half the time the doctor had predicted. The family and close friends could scarcely hide their astonishment. Even the villagers began to talk more kindly of the strange man whom they had mocked behind his back and shunned on the streets.

Regardless of the added burden of his mother's care, van Gogh worked long and hard. His words glowed with color when he wrote to his brother.

Out of doors, everything is mournful; in fact, the fields consist entirely of patches of black earth and snow. Some days one seems to see nothing but fog and mud: in the evening the red sun, in the morning the crows, dried-up grass and withered vegetation, black thickets, branches of poplar stretched against the sad sky like a tangle of barbed wire.

He explained why he studied the peasants and weavers so closely.

I am always searching for blue. As a general rule
the peasants' figures are blue. The people in this
part of the country instinctively wear clothes of the
most beautiful blue color I have seen, made of
coarse cloth which they weave themselves. The
warp is black and the woof is blue, which produces
a combination of black and blue lines. When these
stuffs are faded in tone and discolored with age,
they acquire an extremely soft and subtle shade
which brings out particularly well the color of the
skin.

Van Rappard came again to visit for a short time.
He and van Gogh walked together and enjoyed satisfying talks about their work. This relationship, too,
helped van Gogh with his family and the villagers.
Van Rappard was a gentleman, and people liked
him.

There were other signs as well that perhaps life was
being kinder to van Gogh. Several people began to
call on him in the studio he had set up, for advice and
help in their own artistic efforts.

In Nuenen he found subject matter that suited him.
He loved to visit the cottages of the weavers, for there
he found subjects to challenge his ability. In one cottage, behind a loom of greenish-brown oak standing
against a gray wall, sat a hollow-faced weaver in the
dim lamplight. As the weaver arranged the threads
for the cloth, he threw a pattern of light and shade

upon the wall. The scene fascinated van Gogh, reminding him of the works of Rembrandt. How was he
to transfer this remarkable pattern of light and shade
to his own canvas?

Time and again van Gogh was advised to work
with brighter, more cheerful colors if he wanted to
sell his paintings. He ignored the advice, still preferring the darker tones of the earlier Dutch masters.

Van Gogh fretted, however, at the lack of sales of
his work. His brother had not been able to interest a
single buyer. He realized that there were people who
probably would not like his pictures and said that he
did not care. Yet an artist needs recognition. Van
Gogh suggested to his brother that perhaps he was
not trying hard enough to sell his work. "You seem so
wrapped up with these Impressionists," he complained. He would not be convinced that his brother
was really trying to show his paintings.

Theo van Gogh advised again and again, "Patience.
You are almost saleable."

Such comments goaded van Gogh to fury. "Patience!" he replied vehemently. "For how long must I
go on being patient?" He was tired of being patron-
ized and kept by his father and brother. Finally, out
of all the bickering, they reached an agreement. Van
Gogh would send all the canvases he painted to his
brother in Paris, and in return Theo would give him
an increased allowance. In a sense, Theo van Gogh
was buying his brother's works and could sell them if

he wanted his money back. Now that he was being paid for his paintings van Gogh felt free and his conscience was eased.

Although he had not told anyone yet, there was another reason for van Gogh's lighter spirits. For the first time in his life he had found a real romance. As might be expected, the situation was full of irony and paradox. The episode was tender and joyful, happy and sad—all at the same time.

Next to the van Goghs lived a family named Begemann. Mr. Begemann was an honored member of Pastor van Gogh's church, and the families were close friends. They had even cut a gap in the hedge that separated their two gardens, to make it easier for them to visit each other. A well-worn path lay between the two houses. However, when the van Goghs brought home their incredible son, the visits between the families had grown fewer. Mr. Begemann and van Gogh each disliked the other. This coldness thawed considerably after the artist had nursed his mother during her illness. Then the visits had been resumed, and van Gogh was tolerated by the Begemanns.

Not everyone in the Begemann family, however, was indifferent to him. Margot, a daughter, was a mousy, plain creature. All her natural instincts had been largely smothered by the severe treatment of her puritanical family. She was in her early forties, ten years older than van Gogh, a quiet old maid forever hiding herself in the background. She never had the strength or courage to fight back at the harshness of

PÈRE TANGUY

Paris, 1887　　Musée Rodin, Paris

THE YELLOW HOUSE
(The artist's house)

Arles, 1888   Collection V. W. van Gogh, Laren

her life. But this shy, plain-looking woman began to
show interest in the struggling painter next door. She
smiled at him in a sadly appealing way when no one
was looking.

Forgetting himself for once and feeling sympathy
for this downtrodden creature, van Gogh spoke to
her. She blushed and stammered, but a spark flew
between the ill-starred couple. When van Gogh
showed her his work, he was astounded to discover
that this little nobody, who was hardly ever noticed,
actually understood what he was trying to do. Although Margot had difficulty giving voice to her understanding with this strange man, for the years of
suppression had taken their toll, a friendship took
root and grew between them. She often crossed over
to the van Goghs' garden to watch the artist when he
worked outside. Their relationship was open enough,
but disapproving eyes, from behind unmoving cur-
tains, began to follow her movements.

Saying that she was making her normal rounds of
charity work, Margot was often in the cottages where
van Gogh happened to be working. With a boldness
her family would not have believed she possessed, she
began to accompany van Gogh on his walks about the
countryside. They spent many happy hours together.
Van Gogh had never known such honest companion-
ship with a woman, and he could scarcely believe
what was happening to him. She not only could but
did talk intelligently about his work. Sometimes fear
of her family would cause Margot to become the

strict spinster again. Amazingly, van Gogh understood the reasons for her behavior, so he was able to
remain patient and sympathetic.

Before either of them recognized their feelings,
they were in love. Two lonely, unhappy souls had
found each other.

They made a peculiar-looking couple. Margot was
dowdy, respectability stamped all over her, and van
Gogh, untidy as ever, was always the Bohemian
painter. But they were beautiful to one another.

There was consternation in the Begemann house-
hold over this development. Margot's parents looked
disdainfully on the friendship of their daughter with
the lout that they thought van Gogh to be. They had
no use for him, knowing that he could not support
himself, let alone Margot, but they did not wish to
offend Pastor van Gogh, so for the time being they
kept still. That these two strange human beings were
really in love with each other did not occur to anyone.

Passionately van Gogh wooed Margot Begemann.
He knew she was not a young woman, but he did not
care. "You bring me peace, Margot," he said. "We
must be married, and soon."

Van Gogh knew he could not expect her to change
radically or to embrace his way of living; Margot had
been inhibited far too long. The trappings of respectability could not be stripped away so easily. He
knew he would have to act more in accord with the
demands of society. All right, he could, if he must, be

more conventional. With Margot he could see himself
doing the very things he had always fought against,
for she gave him the strength he needed. With her to
share his life all things were possible.

They agreed to marry, and van Gogh, quite properly, spoke to Margot's father. White-faced, tight with
anger, Begemann stormed at the painter, emphati-
cally refusing to countenance so ridiculous a match.
This reception left van Gogh cold and trembling,
shaking him to his very foundations. The Begemann's
intentions were, in their view, the very best. They did
not realize they were ignoring the deep feelings of
Margot and her suitor.

Margot got an even worse tongue-lashing, and it
was more than her timid spirit could bear. She was
guarded carefully after the proposal, but the first
chance she got she slipped away to see van Gogh. As
they walked in a field, Margot suddenly collapsed to
the ground. At first, van Gogh thought she was merely
exhausted. He lifted her and began to carry her home.
Then some mysterious sense warned him. He looked
at her suspiciously. "Margot," he cried, "you've taken
poison, haven't you?"

In misery Margot nodded bleakly. She was deathly
ill. Van Gogh picked her up and almost ran to the
Begemann house. Begemann took his daughter from
van Gogh, refusing to allow him inside. Margot was
placed in bed, and the doctor was summoned hastily.
She did not die, but the doctor warned her family that
she was in danger of becoming unbalanced if they

continued to treat her as they had in the past. They ignored the warning and sent Margot off to the city of Utrecht. It was six months before she returned to Nuenen.

Vincent poured out his feelings to his brother.

These few days everything else slipped through my mind, I was so absorbed in this sad story. Theo, boy, I am so upset by it. I speak to *nobody* here of it.

I have been to Utrecht to visit the patient; I spent almost the whole day with her. I had an interview with the physician with whom she is staying, because I wanted no other advice than that of a physician about what I must or must not do for the sake of her health and future—whether I must continue our relation, or break it off. According to him, she has always had a very frail constitution; she is too weak to marry, at least now, but at the same time a separation would be dangerous, too. So some time will have to pass before a decision is made. Of course I shall always remain her friend; we are perhaps too much attached to each other.

I think it deeply pathetic that this woman (while yet so weakened and defeated by five or six other women that she took poison) says in a kind of triumph, as if she had gained a victory and had found *rest:* "I too have loved, at last." She had never really loved before.

Before her attempt to kill herself Margot had not been attractive. After her return, she looked a mere ghost. Her nerves had been wrecked. The family shut her up in the house, and van Gogh never saw her again.

The Begemanns left Pastor van Gogh's church and treated the van Gogh family as if they had ceased to exist. The gap in the hedge was closed, and grass grew on the path between the two houses.

Once more Vincent van Gogh had been thwarted. This time the fault was not his; the meddling of others was the cause of the tragedy.

9 *POTATO EATERS*

Van Gogh found little understanding from his own family, for, like the Begemanns, they saw only the incongruity of the ill-assorted couple. They knew nothing of the gentle, tender thing their frail love had been, nor did they try to find out. "Why did you have to interfere with Margot Begemann?" his sister demanded. Van Gogh could see disgust in the faces of all the villagers.

Even his brother was thunderstruck when he heard of the tragic affair. He wrote to van Gogh: "You are so very lacking in concern for Father and Mother. It is so stupid of you to have allowed this to happen. Did you think, for one small moment, what effect all this would have upon the family?"

Only Pastor van Gogh did not criticize, although

the heaviest burden fell upon him. For a short time the congregation of his church grew bigger, the increase simply due to curiosity-seeking gossips who came to view the figures in the tragedy. Then it dropped to nothing.

Perhaps because his father did not openly criticize him, van Gogh attacked everybody within his reach. The pastor, whose whole life's work had gone for nothing, received the worst of his son's violent temper. Van Gogh's reasoning was beyond his family's comprehension. He fell into a mood of despair worse than anything they had dealt with before.

The winter was dreadful. The gloomy man stayed in his studio, shut away from all human contact, and worked on his paintings. Theo van Gogh urged his brother again to move to Paris or a place where he could find other artists with whom he could communicate. "You are too solitary," he wrote. "You are not in touch with what is happening in the world of painting." Nevertheless, van Gogh chose to stay where he was, and somehow the awful winter passed.

Spring brought another blow. Pastor van Gogh had visibly aged during the long winter. Life seemed to have got the better of him. Near the end of March, tired and saddened, he was returning from a walk. As he reached the door of his house he fell to the ground, dead.

At the funeral all the family showed their dislike for his oldest son and kept apart from him even at the graveside. He knew very well that they thought his father's death had been brought on by his tragic relationship with Margot Begemann.

Despite everything, van Gogh was growing enormously in strength and scope as a painter. His figures were coming more and more to life, and he managed to hold onto a few students. Even with them, however, he was the rugged individual, preserving his spirit of independence at all cost. When van Gogh was asked to dinner at one student's house he accepted, but he outraged his hostess by refusing the good meal she had prepared. Instead, he took a piece of bread and sat to one side eating it. "I must never become soft," he said, by way of explanation for his behavior. "I must follow the hard life. Only through suffering can we achieve perfection."

At this time he discovered another idol who stimulated him to a burst of energy. Van Gogh was studying Eugène Delacroix's theories of color and using them, he tried to find a possible connection between color and sound. He took piano lessons, rejecting everything the teacher taught and ignoring all known musical forms. He sat at the instrument, banging away and making the most horrible noises. When he struck a chord he liked, he looked up and shouted to the puzzled teacher, "There! That's a beautiful blue!" But the teacher had seen enough. No wonder they called this awful, uncouth creature the madman of Nuenen. He told his pupil not to come back for any more lessons.

Van Gogh's living conditions faithfully reflected the

conflict in his mind. The two rooms of his studio were littered with rubbish. Dozens of paintings in oils, chalk and watercolor studies, and pencil sketches were strewn all over the room. They stood against walls, were propped up on chairs, and lay in untidy piles on the floors. His big cupboard was overflowing with plants, different kinds of mosses, birds' nests, women's hats, clogs, and odd bits of crockery. Even the chairs were broken, but van Gogh was oblivious to the clutter.

Furthermore, the artist never bothered to clean out his stove. When he made the fire, he simply raked the ashes onto the floor around the stove. After a while almost the entire stove was buried in the pile of ashes. Scattered throughout the unsavory mess were stale crusts of bread he had left lying about. Nothing mattered in the least to him except his work.

Van Gogh gained confidence as his painting improved, but he still had a long way to go. He seldom bothered to sign the pictures he sent off to his brother in Paris. His use of color was not yet fully developed, because van Gogh was still a little afraid of it. He still concerned himself mostly with the drab faces of the peasants he used as models. Their lives were hard and joyless, and the proper way to paint them was in somber colors. From these ideas came a work that brought considerable comment and that began to show his growing strength and unique quality. This study is called *De Ardappeleters* (*Potato Eaters*).

It pictures a group of peasants at their evening

meal. A single lamp lights the scene. The copper browns, the composition, the faces and attitudes of the peasants are ugly, but its power and truth are undeniable. *This* scene comes from life. Theo van Gogh complained that the painting was muddy-looking; others derided it as clumsy. But significantly it was the first one in which van Gogh tried something new. The interior of the peasant cottage he had painted from memory. He had taken seriously Delacroix's advice "to paint by heart."

To his brother he explained: "The colors are those I see through half-closed eyes as I paint. These people reaching for the potatoes I wish to convey as having actually dug the food they are eating. The moral of the picture is the great virtue of manual labor."

Aware of his brother's renewed confidence in him, van Gogh worked long and hard to please him. But a storm was brewing in the village. The first sign was that nobody would come to pose for him anymore, and he soon found out why. A local priest had forbidden his congregation to work for a man he considered an atheist. Moreover, since van Gogh never visited his mother or his sisters, even though they lived nearby, local gossip centered around the possible evil activities in the lonely man's rooms. The artist was told he would have to find accommodations elsewhere, but no one in the village would make room for him. Van Gogh complained to the burgomaster, but to no avail.

While this controversy raged, van Gogh made a short trip to Amsterdam. For a long time he had not

seen the works of any other painters. At the Rijksmuseum he was almost overcome by excitement at
the sight of the paintings. He feasted his eyes and
mind on them. Days when the museum was closed he
sat on its steps, sketching. The activity of the city,
after so long a time in the country, affected him
strongly. He made another trip, this time to Antwerp,
Belgium. From these visits van Gogh learned how
much he had yet to teach himself, but the church ban
was not helping and he could not find another studio.

Back in Nuenen, he gave a painting to one of his
students saying, "Do not worry that it is not signed.
When I am dead my work will be famous." Then
without a word to anyone he left abruptly for Antwerp again. His mother did what she could to clean
his studio, which was in a shambles, and gave away a
group of her son's studies, not wishing to be burdened
with them. The carpenter who received them later
sold them for junk.

Antwerp seemed a paradise to van Gogh. Free of
pettiness and gossip, he felt that he could breathe
once more. He roamed the streets enthralled. The
variety of models and subjects for his brushes was
almost overwhelming. "How could I," he asked himself, "have buried myself away from all this for so
long? Here is what I must have to develop my art."

He rented a small room over a paint store, and soon
he was settled in, painting more rapidly than ever.

10 A GLIMPSE OF THE RAINBOW

In Antwerp the artist forgot the things he had been telling his brother a short time before. In answer to criticism of the dirty coloring of *Potato Eaters,* he had said, "I expect my work to get even darker. I must paint as I see things." Yet van Gogh had caught a glimpse of the rainbow. Ecstatically, he wrote to his brother of his discovery of the excitement in color. "Such blues, such reds!" he cried.

Of equal importance was his discovery of Japanese painting. He found it "gay, full of delicate coloring and form." He loved it so much, he spent every spare penny on Japanese prints, which he hung on the walls of his room. The difference between his work and that of Japanese painters, however, could not have been greater. His was heavy, dark, and thick with paint, in sharp contrast to the fragile beauty of the Oriental paintings.

Van Gogh also discovered Rubens in Antwerp and was captivated by *The Descent From the Cross*. "Rubens fills me with exaltation because he is the one painter who tries to express an atmosphere of joy, serenity, and sorrow by means of a combination of colors," he said. "I am fascinated by the way he expresses the outlines with strokes of pure red and models the fingers of the hands with these same strokes."

Anxiety was never very far from van Gogh, and in Antwerp he worked feverishly, plagued by the thought that he had wasted so much time. He had been painting six years, yet he had not sold anything other than a few drawings. Almost thirty-three years old, he begrudged every moment spent in sleep.

Life in the city was expensive, so he nursed every penny his brother sent him. France was recovering slowly from a severe economic crisis, the effects of which were felt in neighboring countries. Prices had risen since van Gogh had last lived in a big city. Models cost so much to hire that in order to paint he sacrificed all creature comforts. Every franc his brother sent him he spent on paints and art supplies and models. For his food he depended upon what credit he could obtain, giving no thought to how he would eventually pay his bills. In six weeks he ate only three meals that were hot and contained meat. His diet was bread and coffee in the morning and at night. He smoked all the time, hoping the habit would quiet the pangs of his hunger. Somtimes he had a piece of bread at midday when smoking did not help.

Soon enough all the artist's money was gone. So was his credit. For a week he had a morning meal of bread and coffee and nothing else all day long. Now even smoking did not kill the hunger in his stomach. Van Gogh wrote an urgent letter to his brother for money, and an exta bonus arrived. At the first good meal he had, his stomach rebelled, and he could not digest the food. He had pains in his abdomen all the time, and he felt faint. His teeth began to hurt, and some of them broke. All too soon he had gone through the extra money he had received. At this point he painted portraits of himself since he could not afford models, always striving to develop his power and skill.

Nevertheless, van Gogh had to have free models, and there was only one way to get them. He pocketed his pride and applied to the Art Academy in Antwerp, where he would be given free models and free instruction. When Monsieur Verlat, the director, accepted him, van Gogh was relieved. Even though he considered himself a producing artist rather than a student he still needed help.

Older than the rest of the students, van Gogh was an astonishing sight when he turned up for his first class. His round fur cap, almost a trademark, crowned the hollow, hunger-ridden face, from which the light blue eyes darted back and forth restlessly. He wore a butcher's smock, and for a palette he used a piece of wood from an old paint box.

Van Gogh astounded the class even more when he started working, attacking his canvas with speed and vigor unlike anything they had seen. The subject was a pair of wrestlers, naked from the waist up. While the class struggled with this assignment, van Gogh slapped his colors on his canvas so fast and so thickly that paint dropped onto the floor. To the curious students, who cast surreptitious glances at him, the display was incredible. This newcomer seemed to be defying everything they were being taught. Why, the man couldn't even draw properly!

Monsieur Verlat himself conducted the class, and soon he made his rounds of the students' work. Coming to van Gogh, he paused unbelievingly. Verlat, a man in many ways like van Gogh himself, was blunt and to the point when he spoke. "Who are you?" he asked. After van Gogh told him his name, he looked once more at his pupil's work. "That is rubbish," he said. "I have no time for rubbish! You will remove yourself to the class of Monsieur Sieber and take drawing lessons. Now go at once!"

Vincent van Gogh went to Monsieur Sieber's class like a lamb, without a word of protest. Perhaps he respected the director's bluntness. He was told, when he presented himself in the new class, that he must spend at least a year studying and drawing to increase his knowledge of anatomy and work from models in

plaster casts. Once more he made no protest, meekly
submitting to the teacher's instruction. He realized
how much he needed what the academy had to offer
him.

Sieber was a lenient man, yet van Gogh often tried
his patience to the breaking point. Van Gogh believed
the methods taught at the school were wrong. He had
to find truth where *he* saw it and reveal it to others.
When he found instructors incorrect, he exposed
them. Though not yet an Impressionist, he was already a confirmed rebel.

Added to van Gogh's concern about the little time
left to him was another worry. The ghastly thought,
which he strove to thrust from his mind, was fear of
madness. Headaches and nightmares were frequent
and getting more so. Lack of proper food and sleep
were catching up with him again. And his bad teeth
were poisoning his system.

Though van Gogh disliked the conventional instruction offered at the academy, he drew the models
and compositions he was assigned and also sketched
everything else he spied. He drew the other students,
the furniture in the room—in fact, everything. Monsieur Sieber watched him wonderingly, noting his
pupil's speed and impatience, and held his peace.

There were other rebels against conventionality at
the school, and naturally they gravitated around van
Gogh. He was older, bolder, and appeared more sure
of himself than they. This group began to copy his
heavy-handed technique, and, finally, Sieber warned

him that he would have to cease this incitement to rebellion. He was going against all the firm and fixed rules of drawing being taught.

Sieber warned van Gogh again, and they quarreled. Van Gogh retreated. He heeded the warnings as well as he could, for he needed the school badly. But he continued to draw in his own way most of the time.

Money passed through van Gogh's hands with astonishing speed, although he spent it only on his art, allowing himself no pleasures other than his pipe. He wrote his brother constantly, demanding more help. He was worried seriously, too, about his health. A doctor he visited told him that he was on the verge of a breakdown and that he must eat better food and have his teeth cared for. The doctor's advice, of course, went unheeded.

Unable to meet his brother's pleas for more money, Theo van Gogh suggested that he go back home again. He pointed out that, since he had been promoted, he had to do more entertaining of customers, and his own bills grew heavier all the time. Vincent retorted, "Let the bills wait. What are bills to the future of a great artist?" He could not bear the thought of leaving the life he had found in the city despite the hardships. Returning home was an ever more terrifying prospect. Theo suggested that if he went home for a while, he could come to Paris in the summer. The academy would be closing in April. Then they could get together and decide on the future.

Van Gogh did not reach the end of the academic term. The dam of his carefully propped patience gave way. Monsieur Sieber was correcting the class studies of Venus de Milo one day when he saw van Gogh's interpretation of her. It made him gasp. The beautiful figure had become a plump Flemish woman.

"Remember, van Gogh, the unalterable laws of drawing," Sieber said firmly. While he spoke he stroked in correct lines of proportion over his pupil's study of the Venus. Watching his drawing being mutilated, van Gogh trembled with rage, then lost control. He stormed at Sieber, gesturing wildly. "You don't have any idea what a young girl is! They are built that way—the way I draw them—so that they can carry their children!" Angrily he stalked out of the school and never returned.

He explained to his brother why he had left the school. "Always they criticize. 'Draw your outline first, your outline is not right. I shall not correct that if you start modeling before your outlines are complete!' So that's what it comes to. I get on their nerves and they on mine."

Near the end of February, 1886, van Gogh paid his bills by trading some of his paintings, then took a train from Antwerp. On February 27, Theo van Gogh was handed a note where he worked. His brother was outside. He could not wait for summer; he was in Paris now.

Van Gogh was obviously ill and thinner than his brother had ever seen him. His face was lined and drawn, and he was in great pain from his bad teeth. Theo listened to his brother talk excitedly about being in Paris and about the paintings in the gallery. Van Gogh was like an innocent, eager child once again.

When he showed his brother his mouth full of rotten, broken teeth, Theo took him to a doctor. The bad teeth were pulled, and he was fitted with dentures, which improved his looks a little. By the time Theo outfitted him in new clothes, van Gogh looked quite smart, more so, he noticed, than some of the other painters he met. Many of them made a cult of dressing rakishly which they thought marked them as painters and Bohemians, like characters from a comic opera.

The first few weeks in Paris sped by. Theo shared his small apartment on rue Laval with Vincent and enrolled him in the Cormon School of Art. Van Gogh devoured the art treasures of the Louvre and the Luxembourg. He haunted commercial and state art galleries. "Why," he cried to his brother, "one could spend a lifetime studying Rembrandt and Delacroix alone! I ask you, have you ever seen such magical tones as Delacroix's violets and yellows, his blues?"

But Paris was too exciting, too full of other painters for van Gogh to concentrate overlong on Delacroix and Rembrandt. Ever since he had decided to become a painter, he had dreamed of founding a school of painters whose single aim would be to paint life as it was. To his utter amazement, he discovered just such a school flourishing in the very heart of Paris. He had never paid much attention to stories about the Impressionist school. Impressionists were still a long way from recognition. But dealers who looked ahead, who understood the values of art, were beginning to handle their work. Impressionist painters were doing new things with paint and canvas. Their methods, ideas, and objectives were fresh. Impressionism was a whole new concept of painting. Theo van Gogh recognized the trend, but he had trouble trying to convince his employers that they should do business with Impressionist painters.

Van Gogh wrote to an acquaintance he had known in Antwerp. "I didn't know what Impressionism was!" He was enchanted by the lighting effects the Impressionists were getting in their pictures. Light—always the light. "I have seen some of their work," he wrote. "I have not joined them yet, but I hope to do so. I much admire a nude painted by Degas. Also, another painting I like very much is a landscape by Claude Monet."

In some ways van Gogh was a man reborn. His brother wrote to their mother and sisters: "You would hardly know Vincent now. He is in better spirits than I've ever known him. People like him, and he is making great progress in his work. If we can continue together like this, I think the worst difficulties are over. He will make his own way."

Theo van Gogh's own optimism had risen since they

had moved into a new apartment on rue Lepic, in Montmartre, a district long since swallowed up by greater Paris. It was large and airy, and his brother had his own studio room. Both van Goghs were delighted, for the apartment was ideal. They had a commanding view over Paris and around the corner was the Sacre Coeur and countless cafés. A girl came in every day and cleaned the mess Vincent had made.

Van Gogh was overjoyed about their new living conditions. "Paris," he said gleefully, "is my salvation!" His brother, who had never enjoyed robust health, was not feeling his best by any means. Accordingly, he took the line of least resistance, allowing Vincent's enthusiasm to carry him along.

Blissfully, van Gogh went his way. Paris was full of wild spirits like himself, and there were many of them at Cormon's School of Art. Art students, for example, frequently carried revolvers. Van Gogh promptly acquired one.

The artist could not possibly absorb all that Paris had to offer, but he kept trying. He was not calm, but alternated between moods of blithe gaiety and dismay at the enormity of the tasks ahead and his continuing failure to sell his work. Other students at the Cormon School were even stranger than van Gogh, and he gravitated to those who had formed a clique.

Van Gogh was respected at the school as a hard worker and a man of ideas and courage. But he disagreed with Monsieur Cormon. "So he is the head of a

Paris school," van Gogh jeered. "Still he has nothing to say that's worth hearing. He is old-fashioned in his thinking, and, what's more, he holds others back."

Cormon insisted the students take measurements of their studies before starting a picture. Van Gogh thought this method ridiculous. "I never take measurements," he stated flatly.

Cormon replied, "If one doesn't take measurements, one can only draw like a pig!"

Van Gogh was often with the leaders of the school rebels. One of them, a Scot named Alexander Reid, oddly enough looked a little like van Gogh. Van Gogh also became well acquainted with the deformed genius Henri de Toulouse-Lautrec. But the real leader of the rebel art students was a tough-looking, humorous man named Louis Anquetin. Renoir, Degas, Monet, all great painters, were beginning to be recognized, making good money from their canvases. The younger, struggling artists despised them. Van Gogh, his sense of loyalty as strong as ever, could not bring himself to criticize such masters. But the younger ones drew him along. Georges Seurat had invented pointillism, a method of producing luminous effects by filling a canvas with small spots of different colors, which the eye blends into a whole. He, Camille Pissarro, and Paul Signac were the giants of a new generation. They would carry the Impressionist movement forward. The old giants were dead or dying.

At the school Anquetin, now openly painting in the

pointillism technique, made Cormon furious. Cormon had scarcely finished rebuking Anquetin when he discovered Anquetin's cronies doing the same thing. The next student to feel the weight of Cormon's wrath was the young Emile Bernard. Bernard was popular and well liked at the school, and he was a special friend of van Gogh's. They were supposed to be painting a sail, one of the school props, which was a brown color. When Cormon examined Bernard's work he found his painting of this prop was emerging in bands of green and red. "And why, may I ask," he muttered sarcastically, "do you paint a brown sail as red and green bands?"

Bernard snapped back. "Because that is the way I see it!"

"Then, young man, you had better take yourself somewhere else to see things. Leave my school!"

Immediately, protesting groups of students broke up classes. They would no longer tolerate such dictation, such rigidity. They had to express themselves as they saw fit, and van Gogh, always ready for drama, rushed home to get his revolver. He would kill the tyrant! Luckily for van Gogh, when he got back to the school Cormon had vanished.

The school was closed for several months thereafter, and the undisciplined rebel students were frustrated in their wish for action. Then their attention was diverted by a large exhibition of Impressionist painting being held in Paris in May of 1886.

At the exhibition van Gogh was everywhere, gesticulating, a rush of words tumbling from his lips. In his eagerness to express himself, he mixed Dutch, English, German, and French phrases all together. He talked and argued with anyone he could corner. Van Gogh felt a new surge of power as his work drew praise and attention. Alas, with this confidence returned arrogance and intolerance of others who did not see as he saw.

An astonishing transformation had taken place as canvas followed canvas from his easel. A profusion of still lifes caused a good deal of comment. He painted red poppies, blue cornflowers, pink roses, and yellow chrysanthemums. The colors flowed in glowing brilliance, but still he was not satisfied. He painted fish and fruit, but the colors were not bright enough; there was not enough light in his compositions. *The Moulin de la Galette* and *Fishing in the Spring,* painted on the banks of the River Seine, were important works from this time. He painted *Boulevard de Clichy,* the stronghold of his Impressionist friends. One of the most famous of his works appeared, *Montmartre.* It is appreciated now more than it was then, yet there were those who knew that this painting placed Vincent van Gogh's work years ahead of his time. It proclaimed loudly van Gogh's power and originality of conception.

The artist struggled to create ever brighter, cleaner colors. Often he traipsed to the shop of Père Tanguy, on rue Clauzel, where artists bought their paints and supplies. In this shop some of the group's pictures were hung to attract possible buyers. Van Gogh met Paul Cézanne at Tanguy's. Cézanne disliked van Gogh's work and said so. For hours the artists gathered in the shop to discuss color and the merits of various artists, generally ones who were not present. Père Tanguy was an unusual character, and though not an artist himself, he held the respect of these rebellious, argumentative painters. Van Gogh painted him several times, liking the wide red face with its generous red beard.

During the summer months of 1886, van Gogh was pulled and pushed violently by the clashes in Parisian art circles. His love for Japanese art flared up and still brighter colors splashed onto his canvases. The hero of his past was recalled to him when he heard about an exhibition of Millet's work. How different was the style van Gogh was using now.

Tired and weary one day, he took off his boots and dropped them on the floor. The boots, which seemed to have a life of their own, fascinated him, and he stared at them. Worn and dirty as they were, van Gogh could not resist their appeal. He sketched them, then seized his brushes and palette and painted the boots, just as they had been dropped on the floor, in the old dark mood.

11. ENCOUNTER WITH GAUGUIN

"Paris is my salvation!" van Gogh had cried, but he did not guess the dream would fade so soon. In Paris, as always, he progressed from one extreme to another, incapable of finding a happy medium of behavior. He drained every friendship of the last bit of emotion it contained. Heroes and idols followed one another rapidly. He gave no thought to the terrible strain he put on his brother, but the rest of the family saw it each time Theo visited home. They urged him to ask Vincent to move before it was too late. But Theo did not have the heart to turn his brother out of the apartment.

He explained to his mother:

There are two human beings in Vincent, the one extraordinarily gifted, sensitive, and gentle, the other selfish and insensitive. I am sure he is his own enemy, for he poisons not only the lives of others but his own life, yet the seeds of greatness are in him, too.

Van Gogh made no allowance for the fact that his brother was the chief support of the whole family. He refused to understand why there was not unlimited money for his canvases and paints. At one point he dismissed the girl who kept the apartment clean, buying paint with the money so saved.

Also, van Gogh smoked too much, drank too much, and spent too much of his time in cafés. He painted wherever he happened to be and whatever happened to strike his fancy. As a result, the apartment was forever littered with his work. Splashes of paint ruined the floors and the furniture. Van Gogh brought his acquaintances to the apartment at all hours of the night, and they sat up talking and drinking and eating his brother's food, completely ignoring the fact that Theo had to be at work the next day.

Theo grew tired and ill from the excesses. Coping with his brother was problem enough, but since Vincent had more or less taken over the apartment, Theo's own few friends began to drop away. They did not care for the deadly earnestness of van Gogh and his companions.

Instead of finding another place to live, van Gogh found a new place to spend his evenings. It was a fairly new café, called the Café du Tambourin, which, living up to its name, was decorated with tambourines. Owned by Agostina Segatori, an Italian beauty who had modeled for Corot and other painters, the café was a favorite meeting place for artists, poets, and writers. Segatori, closer in age to van Gogh than to many other patrons, instantly took a liking to him. They were an unusual pair—the fierce-looking painter and the dark-eyed, temperamental woman. Perhaps their very difference was what drew them together.

With Lautrec and others van Gogh painted Segatori, and she, to the disgust of a few patrons, hung some of van Gogh's pictures in her café. They were a kind of security for the future, since van Gogh was drinking more all the time and seldom could pay for his drinks. Segatori ignored the complaints about hanging his work in her café.

In the spring of 1887, with his friend Emile Bernard, van Gogh began taking some daily excursions to Asnières, a favorite place for painters not far from the city. Seurat, Monet, Renoir, and Sisley had all painted there. Charmed by the subtle colorings he found, van Gogh was delighted with Asnières. He wrote home:

I am looking for something more than green landscapes and flowers. Last year I painted nothing but flowers to become accustomed to using colors. I painted pinks, soft and glaring green, light blue, violet, yellow and orange and a beautiful red. Now, painting at Asnières, I see more colors than ever before.

Van Gogh found the French sky "delicate and clear, quite different from the sky of Le Borinage, which was close and foggy." He began to long for hot cloudless skies with strong sunshine, thinking that color would be much more true in such an atmosphere. But he would only be able to find it in the South.

The painter, Signac, joined van Gogh and Bernard at Asnières for a while. Signac had a fine sense of humor and was amused by van Gogh's painting habits, but he also had a healthy respect for the man and his work. Of the artist, Signac later said, "He loved life passionately; he was ardent and good."

They painted beside the river on the outskirts of Paris until it grew dark, then walked back to the apartment on rue Lepic. Signac described van Gogh working beside him. "Van Gogh, in his blue butcher's coat, had painted dots of color on his sleeves. Standing close to me he bawled and gesticulated, waving his large wet, freshly painted canvas. He smeared himself and anybody who came near him with all the colors of the rainbow."

At this time van Gogh was painting great masses of yellow sunflowers, finding their mass and color fascinating, and he also painted *Wheatfield with Lark*.

Gradually van Gogh began to realize that the charm he had found in the city was fading. The spell in Asnières had made him aware that he was becoming cramped in the big city, and he was growing tired of too much smoking, too much talking, too much carousing. Furthermore, van Gogh began to see that beyond all the excitement and stimulation of Paris there was destructiveness. The bright talk and the discussions of new ideas and techniques contained germs of gossip, bitterness, envy, and malice. Often life became a vicious circle of personality clashes and quarrelings about insignificant things. Van Gogh was uneasy as he grew more aware of the situation.

The spring and summer outings increased the artist's desire to move south. There he could find light. Clarity and freshness would come to his colors. And he was dreaming a dream. Could he start a Southern school of painting that would excel in the light and power of its work? Paul Gauguin had talked so, too.

Gauguin, the idol of a Paris clique, not only talked of what he wished to do, he did it. He had wandered all over South America, and when he returned to Paris he regaled his friends with tales of his adventures. He also brought back paintings with colors such as they had never seen. He said that they were due to the clarity of the light in tropical lands. But he told nothing of the severe hardships he had suffered during these travels. Van Gogh listened and watched.

During the summer of 1887 van Gogh painted a "yellow" work, which he called *Parisian Novels*. It created a sensation among painters, drawing respect and praise for its creator, but van Gogh could not sell it. An English acquaintance, A. S. Hartrick, was impressed by the painting, but less impressed with the painter. In sparse language he commented about him with great penetration. "He is simple as a young child, expressing pain and pleasure loudly!"

Again, van Gogh quarreled with everyone. His heavy drinking made him depressed and even touchier than usual. He fell out with Segatori, and when he tried to collect his paintings, she reminded him of their value as her security for his unpaid bills. In moments of clarity van Gogh knew how mercilessly he abused his brother, but he thrust such thoughts from his mind, unable to bear contemplating them. He used his old trick of hiding his faults and weaknesses by attacking others. Headaches and nightmares became frequent again.

Overhearing van Gogh make a caustic remark about Segatori at the Café du Tambourin, a new favorite of hers attacked van Gogh and threw him, covered with blood, from the café. His confusion and his ugliness made him look menacing, and he was called mad openly. Models refused to pose for him.

To overcome this problem, he took his easel and paints into the streets of Paris. The gendarmes, however, made him move on, for he was disturbing the peace, and thus they cut off his access to free models. Van Gogh scuffled with the gendarmes several times, and he frequently embarrassed his brother at the gal-

lery where he worked. The police often brought
Vincent to Theo, who then had to pacify both par-
ties.

Returning in November from a stay in Martinique,
Gauguin was again in Paris. Gauguin had several
things in common with van Gogh. He, too, had come
to the realization of his genius late in life, which, as
with van Gogh, gave him a sense of insecurity. Time
was vital to both. Gauguin was a giant among painters, but as a man he was widely disliked and feared,
almost as much as van Gogh. Completely dedicated
to his art, he had thrown over a successful business on
the Paris Stock Exchange and had abandoned his wife
and children to follow his passion. These well-adver-
tised facts did not endear him to more responsible
people. Gauguin, however, cared nothing for what
others thought of him.

To be close to Gauguin, one had to worship at his
feet. Through Emile Bernard van Gogh met the
painter. Gauguin paid little attention to him, but van
Gogh admitted to himself that Gauguin had greater
powers than he.

Gauguin believed that the future of painting lay in
the true civilization of primitive lands where life was
unspoiled, and van Gogh fed upon Gauguin's talk of
"returning to nature." Time after time van Gogh listened to Gauguin's description of the incredibly pure
atmosphere in the tropics, which gave colors a startling effect. There were also plenty of models, for the
native people were only too happy to pose for free.

GAUGUIN'S CHAIR

Arles, 1888   Collection V. W. van Gogh, Laren

POSTMAN ROULIN

Arles, 1889   Rijksmuseum Kröller-Müller, Otterlo

Gauguin tolerated van Gogh because Theo was trying to sell some of his paintings at the gallery. However, when van Gogh ventured to air his own views to this master painter of the future—which he believed Gauguin to be—he got quick and bitingly sarcastic answers. Gauguin smashed all his heroes such as Mauve. Although van Gogh did not abandon his loyalties, he surrendered to Gauguin's arguments. After all, he reasoned, he was in the presence of a man several years older and vastly more experienced.

The two artists made a strange pair. Van Gogh was small-framed, animated with nervous agitation. Gauguin was a big man with greenish eyes glaring from a face browned by tropic sunshine and seamed by hardships. Gauguin wore wooden shoes, fishermen's trousers and jersey, and a beret. A pipe was always stuck in the corner of his mouth. His attitude toward others was aloof and dictatorial, and he seldom tried to conceal his contempt for lesser painters. Yet he had an overall calmness that contrasted dramatically with van Gogh's spasmodic speech and jerky movements.

Early in 1888 van Gogh became disgusted with the Paris scene. Claude Monet refused to let his pictures hang in any place showing Gauguin's. Renoir, Seurat, and Signac were at odds with one another. Van Gogh, who was himself seldom secure, felt that the artists were destroying one another. Accordingly, he approached Gauguin with his idea of founding a school of painting in the south of France, explaining that with Gauguin advising, directing, and setting the standards they must succeed.

Although Gauguin admitted willingly enough that van Gogh was highly gifted, he wanted no part of this plan. To him, Vincent van Gogh was too unstable and would prove an impossible companion in such a venture.

And so van Gogh continued to carouse with Toulouse-Lautrec, drinking more than was good for him, trying to lose himself for a while by painting even more furiously. Dreaming of the sun in the South, of the colors he could create in the pure light there, van Gogh was near to despair. He felt like a prisoner in Paris now.

12 THE YELLOW HOUSE ∎

Again Theo van Gogh saved his brother's sanity. One day Theo took him to Seurat's studio. Most of van Gogh's acquaintances had long since ceased to have anything to do with him. Seurat, however, did not belong to this group. He was a serious man with sound ideas, and van Gogh liked him. Fortunately, the meeting brought van Gogh out of his black mood. Talking and discussing ideas with Seurat gave him much pleasure. With him, there was none of the heavy drinking that had been van Gogh's outlet for too long.

Seurat insisted that the future of painting did not lie with any one artist nor with artists all going their own way. The painter had a duty to present beauty and truth to his fellow men. Illustrating his meaning to van Gogh with his own large canvases, he said:

These paintings are not playthings for the rich. Rather they should be used to decorate walls for the pleasure and benefit of all. Work like this should be used to beautify public buildings where all can enjoy it.

If there could be a communal fund from which all painters could be paid it would remove much of the poverty we suffer. Just enough to live decently. It could be arranged that canvases and paints and brushes would be guaranteed to everybody who joined the project. Painters could find their inspiration in the joy of working toward a common end that would enrich the lives of all. Such a group, you know, could beautify our civilization as the Greeks beautified theirs.

Van Gogh was enthusiastic. Seurat was defining a purpose beyond one's selfish needs. This same dream, of painters working together, he had dreamed himself. Seurat's words comforted him and made him feel that he had been right all along.

Because he was the giant among them, Gauguin should be the leader. But, van Gogh wondered, if I gather a group of painters who will live up to the ideas and standards Seurat described, can I then possibly persuade Gauguin to take over its leadership?

Next day, he called on his friend Bernard. Together they straightened the mess van Gogh had made in Theo's apartment, and, feeling warm toward his brother, van Gogh carefully arranged his paintings on the walls. Then he left Paris, planning to make his way down to Marseilles on the south coast.

The artist did not reach Marseilles. As he journeyed south, he was enthralled by the rainbow of colors he saw. The sky was limpid, and there seemed to be a sparkle in the air such as he had never seen, except possibly in the Japanese paintings he loved. In child-like wonder he described his delight.

I noticed a magnificent landscape of enormous yellow rocks twisted into the most fantastic shapes. I saw wonderful red fields planted with vines, with a delicate background of purple mountains in the distance. And the snowy landscapes, with white peaks set against a sky as luminous as the snow, remind me of winter landscapes in Japanese art.

Near the end of February van Gogh reached Arles, an ancient Roman town in Provence. After strolling around, he fell in love with it and decided to stay. Quickly he found lodgings on rue Cavaleré. A thick snow was on the ground, but the sky above was a deep, sparkling blue. The Roman ruins there did not interest him, but everything else did. The Arlésiennes as the people of Arles were called especially intrigued

him. Van Gogh began to paint and worked cease-
lessly. The bright sunlight, reflecting from the snow,
hurt his eyes, but he reveled in the landscape.

Spring came and the snows vanished. Day after day
he painted in the fields or around the town. He
worked long hours outdoors, fearful that the beauty
around him would escape his brush.

The mistral, a violent, cold, dry northeast wind,
capable of hurling good-sized stones, started blowing
without pause. Covering his canvases with a fine coat-
ing of dust, the wind added a great burden to van
Gogh's already overtaxed mind. But he worked on.
Sometimes he was forced to hang onto his canvas
with one hand, painting awkwardly with the other. As
the wind grew stronger and whipped at his canvas,
smearing the wet paint as he applied it, van Gogh
pegged his easel to the ground. When necessary, he
left his easel and painted on the ground, kneeling on
his canvas to hold it firm. He felt as if the mistral were
full of malice and spite, directed at him personally,
and his determination equaled its strength.

As summer came, the sun blazed daily in a cloudless sky, and van Gogh relished its warmth and its
golden light. Although the hot sun, burning down on
top of his head, was dangerous, van Gogh was oblivious of taking any risk. Every day he painted in feverish haste. Canvas after canvas glowed with a warm
yellow and riotous colors.

In excitement and wonder he wrote to his brother
of his impressions. "We are now enjoying glorious hot

weather, which is just right for me. Sun and light! Which, for want of a better word, I can call yellow, pale saffron yellow, pale golden lemon—how beautiful the yellow is!"

He also wrote to Emile Bernard about his work.

I apply my brushstrokes quite unsystematically. I lay the paint freely on the canvas with irregular strokes, which I leave as they are. Here is a sketch of the entrance to a Provence orchard, with its yellow fences, its shields of cypresses against the mistral, and its vegetables of different greens, yellow lettuce, green onions, and emerald leeks. Although I work on the spot, I try to seize what is essential in the design. I fill up spaces with a uniform simplified tone in such a way that everything which is to be ground will share the same violent tone. The whole sky will be of a blue tone.

The clarity of the atmosphere revealed colors that were entirely different from those in the darker Northland he knew so well. "Down here," he wrote, "the color scheme at the moment is rich with azure, orange, pink, vermilion, glaring yellow, green, wine-red, and violet. But tranquility and harmony arise out of the use of all these colors."

Van Gogh was quite happy at first. "What an opportunity!" he wrote. "Nature here is so extraordinarily beautiful. It's the chance of a lifetime! I feel a different man from the one who came here. I let myself go, paint what I see and just how I feel—and hang the rules!"

When he was not painting, however, van Gogh was lonely, for he had made no friends. As usual, he had very little money, and he sacrificed food and personal comforts for paints and supplies. Moreover, the strain of hard work, his constant struggle against the mistral, and lack of nourishment took its toll of his strength. The artist's body became a mass of screaming nerves. He knew he must rest for a while. If he did, he reasoned, he would be ready to paint again when summer was in full bloom.

At this time news reached him of the death of Anton Mauve. Again he felt depressed over the passing time. Trying to be philosophical, he wrote, "I can't think that people like Mauve cease to exist after death. Perhaps there will be something after that."

During this period of enforced rest, his loneliness increased. Van Gogh disliked the inn where he stayed, and he was not eating properly. Although he blamed the innkeeper's poor food for his bad health, the rebellion in his stomach was the real cause of his trouble.

He told his brother:

Here the wine is bad, but I drink very little of it. And so it comes about that, with eating hardly any and drinking hardly any, I am pretty weak. You know, if I could only get really strong soup it would do me good straight off: it's preposterous,

but I *never* can get what I ask for, even the sim-
plest things from these people here.

But it is not hard to cook potatoes?

Impossible.

Then rice, or macaroni?

None left, or else it is messed up in grease, or else
they aren't cooking it today and they'll explain that
that's tomorrow's dish, there's not room on the
range, and so on. It's absurd, but that's the real
reason why my health drags along.

Awareness of the dangers ahead was sometimes
very clear to van Gogh, and he often wrote to Emile
Bernard of his torment.

If I reflect, I think of the possibilities of disaster,
then I can do nothing. So I throw myself body and
soul into my work, and my paintings are the result
of this effort. If the storm inside me growls too
loudly, I drink a glass too much to stun myself.
This is madness when I consider what I ought to
be.

Not only my pictures, but also I myself have recently become haggard, like Hugo van der Goes in
the picture by Emile Wauters. But I think that having carefully had my beard shaved off, I resemble
the calm abbot in that picture as much as the mad
painter who is so cleverly represented. And I am
not sorry to be a mixture of the two, because we
must live, and because there is no getting away

from the fact that one day or another there may be
a cataclysm.

Still, van Gogh dreamed often of his school of
painters and hoped that before long Gauguin would
join him in this painter's paradise. He began to look
for a place of his own and rented a studio at the
corner of Place Lamartine. He loved the small house,
which had two rooms downstairs and two above. It
was yellow with a green door, and inside the walls
were white, the floors tiled red. Van Gogh knew
somehow he must have it for his own. "How lovely
my paintings will look stacked along the white walls.
A perfect background for their bright colors!"

Unfortunately, by the time he had bought a table
and two chairs and a few utensils his money was
gone. Since he had no bed, he could not live in his
house all the time. He was delighted with it, however,
after he got his pictures arranged, and when the
weather was bad he worked inside. He tried to buy a
bed, hoping to pay for it a little at a time, but nobody
would give him credit.

Absorbed in the bursting life around him, van Gogh
was totally unaware of the impression he was making.
He did not notice that people were beginning to look
at him with distaste. They found this odd-looking
man in their midst most peculiar, and some commented openly that he was mad. So devoted to his
painting had he been that his personal appearance
was dreadful. Thus, the gossip began to spread.

Once van Gogh had his little house arranged to his liking, he painted everything in it. Many of these works show his fascination with yellow. Some of his best still lifes were painted at this time, but soon he wearied of them. He wanted human flesh-and-blood models. Unfortunately, he had no money to pay for them and when he asked others to pose he was invariably turned down. The townspeople were afraid of the fierce-looking painter. When he took his easel into the streets hoping to get free models, he met with hostile curiosity. Children ran after him, taunting and calling nasty things to him. Although the artist ignored them as well as he could, nevertheless he was hurt.

In frustration over the lack of models van Gogh made several more self-portraits. Without his beard his face looked narrower, more ferretlike than ever. These pictures show with startling clarity the remarkable story of a tormented soul. Finally, he found a human model. A young Zouave agreed to pose for him. This colorful North African soldier was a delightful subject. His red fez, embroidered jacket, and balloonlike pantaloons made a most pleasing combination. "This lad," van Gogh wrote, "has a small face, the neck of a bull, and the eyes of a tiger."

Regardless of obstacles, van Gogh's determination pushed him on. He told Emile Bernard about the house and about his work, describing graphically the delightful scenes around him. No doubt he reminded himself that Bernard was always with Gauguin and

that, in some way, these comments might help persuade Gauguin to come and see for himself. He wrote
about a landscape he was working on.

Of the town you can see only a few red roofs and
a tower. The rest is hidden by the green of fig trees
in the background and a narrow strip of sky above.
The town is surrounded by vast fields containing
endless buttercups like a yellow sea. In the fore-
ground these fields are intersected by ditches full
of purple irises. They cut the grass just as I was in
the middle of painting it, so I only have a study
instead of a finished picture. But what a subject!

Van Gogh decided to make his way down to the
Mediterranean, which he had never seen before.
Walking along the beach at Saintes-Maries de la Mer,
he found a subject that he could not resist. A group of
gaily painted fishing boats were pulled up on the
sand. He painted them on the beach and also floating
on the crystal blue water.

Van Gogh would have liked to stay longer by the
sea. At night the dark-blue, soft sky, sprinkled with
brilliant twinkling stars, enchanted him. But the
bloom of summer and the promise of the astonishing
fertility of harvesttime called him back to Arles.

Van Gogh was still horribly lonely back in Arles.
To ease his pain he began to drink again, sitting by
himself in the cafés. In the hot summer mornings he
went out to paint and stayed all day long. The work-

ers sensibly returned to rest during the midday heat, but van Gogh sat, solitary, painting to the exclusion of all else. At dusk he made his way wearily back to town and, without eating, settled down with a drink. The routine was damaging.

Then he even started painting during the night, trying to reproduce the velvety dark tones dotted with silver stars. He fastened a candle to the brim of his straw hat and sat for hours, trying to put his feelings onto his canvas.

Exhausted in mind and body by the furious pace at which he pushed himself, Vincent was bound for trouble. He suffered dreadful headaches, nervousness, and pains in his stomach. Foreboding, odd remarks began to creep into his letters to Theo. The taunting urchins in the streets did their mean part in preventing the artist from finding peace of mind, and the people of the town remained hostile toward him. Willpower alone kept him going. "I'm entirely incapable of judging my work," he told his brother. "I can't see whether my studies are good or bad."

Van Gogh managed to drag himself through the days when he was painting. When he did not paint, his weak condition, his loneliness, and his tormenting thoughts kept his brain in a whirl. In a town full of people, there were days when not a soul spoke a word to him. Sickly looking touches of yellow and green appeared in some of his paintings, reflecting the sickliness in his mind. Sometimes he was terribly aware of the presence of doom. "I have a body that's good for nothing and a mind near enough mad to make no matter," he cried bitterly.

And always the mistral bothered him. With his nerves shrieking, his mind whirling, he exclaimed, "That devil mistral!" He began to pester his brother in his letters to put pressure on Gauguin to join him at Arles. Gauguin was in Brittany, ill with a liver ailment. He, too, was appealing to Theo van Gogh for money. Theo sent his brother what he could spare, and he also told him of Gauguin's condition. Van Gogh's hopes soared. Surely Gauguin would see the sense of coming to Arles. "You cannot afford to keep him in Brittany and keep me here in Arles at the same time," he wrote cunningly. "Why does he not come here? For about 250 francs a month we could both live and work here and the drain would not be too hard on you."

Theo promised to see what he could do to persuade Gauguin of this plan. He knew the terror of his brother's loneliness, and he seriously thought the idea had merit. Van Gogh could learn much from Gauguin, and Gauguin could profit from the better climate and wider range of subject matter. Unable to restrain himself and leave matters to his capable brother, van Gogh wrote Gauguin himself. In exchange for supporting them, they could give their work to his brother. If he sold it, that would be fine.

When Theo broached the matter, Gauguin reluctantly agreed to the idea. But he begged off an immediate departure, complaining that he had not enough

money for the fare. Gauguin was a bitter man. He had
a good reputation for his work, but he could not sell
enough of it to live decently. He was often close to
starvation and suffered frequently from the humilia-
tion of having to beg and borrow materials for his
work. Unlike van Gogh, Gauguin did not believe that
suffering such hardships was necessary in order to be
a better painter. In this unhappy state, he let matters
drift once he had verbally agreed to go to Arles.

The news that Gauguin was joining him greatly
stimulated van Gogh. Ideas and notions poured out in
his letters. "It would make a big difference to me if
Gauguin comes," he wrote. "Left to oneself for too
long in the country one becomes stupid. When he
comes there'll be plenty of talk, plenty of ideas. And
if we make up our minds not to quarrel we shall help
each other to increase our reputations." Van Gogh
hoped also to persuade Emile Bernard to stay with
them.

By July of 1888, Gauguin still had not arrived in
Arles. Van Gogh grew anxious. The house needed better furnishings. While his brother paid the rent, he had
no money to spare to buy beds and other essentials.
Then Theo had a stroke of luck; Uncle Vincent died
and left him some money. Once, Vincent had been his
intended heir, but in his will Uncle Vincent had made
no mention of him.

Theo sent the news to his brother, telling him that
as soon as he received the money, he would send it all
to Vincent. With it he could rent the house for as long

as he wanted and furnish it. Having softened the blow somewhat, he warned his brother: "Do not depend too much upon Gauguin's coming to Arles. He might decide not to come, and even if he does, he may prove a lot more difficult to live with than you seem to think." He suggested to his brother that perhaps he should join Gauguin in Brittany, reminding him that his friend Bernard was there, too.

Summer passed. September came. Still no Gauguin. But Gauguin was being forced to a decision by considerations other than Vincent van Gogh's desires. He had worked hard and well all summer. Now he faced a long dreary winter. He had not sold any paintings although Theo had managed to sell some pottery Gauguin had made. The other artists who had spent the summer in Brittany were going back to their city studios, and the countryside was getting cold and miserable. Still, Gauguin hesitated to go to Arles.

Finally Gauguin convinced himself that he should accept the invitation, and he wrote Theo for money for his fare.

Immediately after Theo van Gogh sold one of Gauguin's paintings for five hundred francs, but before the money reached Gauguin in Brittany, he had left for Arles. Hopefully, Theo wrote his brother about the sale. At least, Gauguin would not be entirely without funds of his own. He sent the money on to the yellow house.

Very late at night, toward the end of October, Gauguin arrived in Arles.

13· THE EDGE OF MADNESS

By this time van Gogh was sleeping at the yellow house. The hour was so late that Gauguin decided not to call immediately, so he spent the rest of the night sitting at a café. As soon as it was light, he set off for Place Lamartine. Van Gogh was bleary-eyed when he answered the door, but he soon woke up when he saw who was calling at so early an hour.

Nervous and excited, happy and anxious all at once, he showed Gauguin the house where they were to work and, he hoped, start a school of dedicated painters. He had worked hard to make Gauguin's room attractive, and it did look nice. When van Gogh showed him the studio where he himself painted, it was a dreadful litter of paints, brushes, and canvases. Gauguin was a fastidious man and a practical one in many respects. He whipped off his jacket and set to work with a will. Van Gogh was astonished. In practically no time Gauguin had turned the dirty kitchen into a gleaming place of order where food could be cooked and served cleanly. Obviously where such things were concerned van Gogh was hopeless. If Gauguin was to live with this strange man, he would have to take charge. Accordingly, he at once set up a housekeeping system. There was a box for food money and another for rent.

The peace and order Gauguin brought with him to the yellow house worked wonders for van Gogh, and the first few days passed rapidly. Regular food and consistent working hours created a miracle, and he looked many times better. Before his very eyes, van Gogh believed he saw his dream of a painters' colony coming true. Furthermore, the man he so badly wanted to lead this group was actually there, living and working in the yellow house! Van Gogh had seldom known such contentment. He did not mind that Gauguin got along so much better in town than he did. Women found the big, dark painter much more attractive than the small, thin redhead. Nevertheless, van Gogh was satisfied that they worked together and that he had Gauguin to talk with and to learn from, and he learned much.

Gauguin was deeply impressed with the progress of van Gogh's painting. He keenly appreciated the power and originality of van Gogh's conceptions, and he did not withhold his opinions. Van Gogh basked in the praise of this man he admired and loved so much.

Theo van Gogh must have been very relieved that, despite his misgivings, his brother's scheme seemed to be off to a good start. Undoubtedly he prayed that it would continue so, for he had affairs of his own he wished to concentrate on. He had been courting Johanna Bonger, the sister of one of his close friends, and they were preparing to marry. Theo's hope was that since his brother was so wrapped up with Gauguin and his painting there would be no scenes over his marriage to Johanna.

While all was well on the surface, Theo may well have momentarily felt alarmed when he received a troubled letter from his brother.

Just now I am not ill, but I should get ill without the slightest doubt if I did not take plenty of food, and if I did not stop painting for days at a time. As a matter of fact, I am pretty nearly reduced again to the madness of Hugo van der Goes. And if it were not that I have almost a double nature, as it were of a monk and of a painter, I should have been reduced, and that long ago, completely and utterly to the condition aforesaid. Yet even then I do not think that my madness could take the form of persecution, since my feelings when in a state of excitement lead me rather to the consideration of eternity, and eternal life.

After putting the house in order, Gauguin naturally tried putting his companion's thinking in order. As they worked, talked, and lived together, Gauguin became appalled at van Gogh's mind, which appeared to be cluttered with odd bits of information, unrelated values, and confused opinions on art and artists.

"Free your imagination," Gauguin told him. "You have a talent for the abstract. Paint from memory. You do not need models as much as you think you do. We must avoid meaningless photographic reproduction in our work. What we should do is go back to the clear-eyed lack of prejudice as in children."

Van Gogh, the great resister, absorbed these new thoughts and ideas like a dry sponge. Coming from the lips of the man Gauguin, who was everything to him, van Gogh believed the comments and suggestions about his work and ideas the greatest wisdom.

Gauguin found van Gogh a willing pupil, now calm and quiet, and the peace he was enjoying showed in his work. Paintings of objects in the house—everything from the coffeepot to the beds—were coming from his easel, surely and beautifully. He drew his chair and Gauguin's, and in some mysterious way, even though the chairs were empty, he seemed to get each man's personality into his own chair. One looked as if it was used by a heavier person than the other.

At times van Gogh had blinding flashes of self-awareness. He wrote to his brother from Arles.

I cannot help it that my pictures do not sell. The time will come when people will see that they are worth more than the price of the paint and my own living—very meager, after all—that are put into them. But, my dear lad, my debt is so great that when I have paid it, the pains of producing pictures will have taken my whole life from me, and it will seem to me then that I have not lived.

And so, in blissful contentment, the first weeks passed. But a man's character formed over the years does not change overnight. The other van Gogh—the contentious, disagreeable, unpleasant one—lay in wait, ready to destroy his newfound happiness and success. Moreover, Gauguin was not the god van Gogh considered him to be. Men make gods of other men at their peril. Gauguin was very human, and his irritations grew as van Gogh asserted himself.

At the end of six weeks the golden dream was already fading. The hot yellow sun van Gogh loved to paint was being crowded off his canvas by an approaching black, worse than anything he had ever endured. He and Gauguin were quarreling.

"Gauguin and I talked a lot about Delacroix and Rembrandt," he wrote. "Our arguments are terribly *electric;* we come out of them sometimes with our heads as exhausted as an electric battery after it is discharged."

The trouble was partly of Gauguin's own making.

He had invaded some of his companion's most hallowed ideals, harshly and cruelly trampling on them. He attacked the men van Gogh had worshiped for years, and he bitingly criticized van Gogh's own work in some cases. Always quick to flare at criticism, whether real or imagined, van Gogh began to seethe with unspoken resentment. And intensely personal scathing arguments resulted. They disagreed violently on who was the greatest painter. Van Gogh began to suffer more severe headaches again, and his nervousness became worse than ever. For a while he wavered. He began to see dimly that this man he adored was not a superman. Then he might revert suddenly, for a day to his earlier fanatic adoration. The situation was one that had to explode eventually.

Gauguin began to stay away from the house as much as he could. On his return, van Gogh was waiting to start the arguments, in which he took a fiendish delight, all over again. Then the tormented artist would go to the other extreme, becoming silent and morose, uttering not a word all day.

Twice Gauguin wakened to find van Gogh menacingly creeping toward his bed. "What are you doing, Vincent? What is the matter?" Gauguin asked.

Van Gogh crept back to his own room like a man in a trance. Gauguin wrote Theo and asked him for fare back to Paris. "We are too different in temperament," he told him. "We cannot live peaceably together here. We are so completely incompatible."

When van Gogh learned of this request, his attitude changed completely. He pleaded with Gauguin, begging him to stay. Gauguin softened and agreed, not really relishing the winter cold and uncertainty of Paris.

One day van Gogh gazed upon a finished portrait Gauguin had made of him. Silently he regarded his own likeness as seen through Gauguin's eyes. "Yes," he said finally. "It's me all right! But it's me *mad!*"

The two men left the house together and went into a café. The instant he was served, van Gogh threw his drink at Gauguin. He missed. Without speaking Gauguin rose from the table, took van Gogh's arm, and led him home. He placed him on his bed where the artist, unspeaking, unmoving, seemed like one dead.

"I am very sorry," van Gogh said next morning. "I didn't know what I was doing." He talked of the pains in his head.

"The damage is done, Vincent," Gauguin replied. "Had your drink splashed me I am sure I should have hit you. That, my friend, would not have helped either of us. Once is enough! It is better that I leave here and return to Paris."

Gauguin's calm determination shocked van Gogh into a renewed plea that Gauguin stay. "You need the peace here to work. Where else can you find it?"

"Peace you say? What peace has there been in this house recently?" Gauguin demanded.

Van Gogh watched Gauguin sort out his possessions preparing to leave. Surely he would not go. Yet everything Gauguin was doing indicated that he would. For two days van Gogh, his mind in a terrible state of turmoil, watched Gauguin like a hawk. Then, two days before Christmas, 1888, thirty-five-year-old Vincent van Gogh broke down completely.

Gauguin was crossing the street in front of the yellow house. The evening was quiet, and every sound seemed exaggerated. Suddenly he heard footsteps and, recognizing them, Gauguin turned. A horrified look crossed his face. Van Gogh was coming at him with an open razor in his hand. With his wits working furiously, Gauguin spoke loudly. "What are you up to?"

Without a word, van Gogh turned and fled into the house. He stood for a long time gazing at himself in the mirror, the open razor still in his hand. What torment was in his collapsing brain only he could ever know. Suddenly he lifted his hand and, in a lightning movement, cut off part of his right ear with the razor. Tying a scarf around his head to stop the profuse bleeding of the ear he had mutilated, he crammed his round fur hat down on his head, picked up the severed piece of his ear, and put it in an envelope. Then he left the house.

Van Gogh walked to the noisy part of town where the African Zouaves and others who liked late hours gathered. He saw a girl he knew slightly and gave her the envelope containing the piece of his ear. She opened it, screamed, and fell in a faint.

Instantly a crowd gathered. The fierce-looking Zouaves fingered their African daggers. Van Gogh stood in the midst of the surging throng of yelling women, soldiers, and civilians. Blood covering him, he was a fearful sight. Before the police could arrive, a man who delivered the artist's mail led him away from the mob, took him home, and put him to bed. Gauguin stayed away all that night, afraid to go back to the yellow house in fear of his life.

Next morning, when Gauguin arrived to get his things and leave for Paris, a large crowd had gathered at the front of the house. Several gendarmes were keeping the crowd in check. Inside, the house was covered with blood. Van Gogh was on his bed, unconscious. The gendarmes were questioning everybody, trying to find out what had happened. Gauguin told them quickly that he had spent the night away from the house and had nothing to do with this awful thing. They let him go, and at once he sent a telegram to Theo, telling him to come to Arles immediately.

14 DARK DAYS

When the message reached Theo van Gogh in Paris, he was about to leave with his wife Johanna on a trip to Holland to visit relatives. He sent his wife on northward, but he took the earliest possible southbound train.

Gauguin met him at the station in Arles. "Vincent is very ill in the hospital," he told Theo. "He has finally lost control over his mind and actions." White-faced and anguished, Theo listened to Gauguin's story.

"How is he now?" he asked.

"I don't know, Theo," Gauguin said. "I have been afraid to visit him. I think my presence might only make matters worse."

Theo went quickly to Vincent's bedside. In this

awful moment there was a greatness in the love of
these two brothers for each other. Theo laid down his
head on the bed beside his brother's, and this gesture
seemed to bring the artist comfort. His eyes, which
had been open and staring since he had been brought
to the hospital, mercifully closed.

Before long van Gogh opened his eyes again, and
this time they were not so agonized. He seemed to be
struggling, however, against an iron grip he could not
break. Even the relief of shedding tears was denied
him. He could only suffer his pain like a dumb animal.

At this point van Gogh felt hopeless. The struggles,
the disappointments, the hurts, the brief moments of
happiness—everything was swallowed up by the
blackness. Although his heart was full of love to give,
all that came to him was trouble. Even the knowledge
of the beauty he had created in his paintings could
not comfort him at this moment.

The great loss of blood had weakened the artist
visibly. His recovery—if he made one—would be
slow. "If Vincent should die," his brother said sadly,
"it would break my heart." Nevertheless, Theo had no
choice but to return to Paris. At least, he left with the
assurance of knowing the doctor who cared for his
brother was a good man and would keep him informed of Vincent's progress.

Gauguin rode in the train with Theo to Paris. He
knew he shared some of the blame for the tragedy.

"But what could I have done?" he asked. "I know that trying to see him in the hospital would have excited him and made things worse."

Somewhat surprisingly, Theo did not hold a grudge against Gauguin. Apparently he felt that this awful thing was bound to happen, and Gauguin, after all, had done much for his brother's good. Van Gogh himself, in all his misery, maintained stoutly how much he owed to Gauguin.

By early 1889 van Gogh was reported out of danger. Immediately he began agitating to get back to his house and continue with his painting. He felt that he had little time left for the work he wanted to do. Although afraid of another breakdown, he referred to his bout of mental illness sparingly.

I hope I have been the victim of nothing worse than an artist's prank. It astonishes me when I compare my condition with what it was a month ago. I knew that one could fracture one's legs and arms and recover, but I did not know you could fracture the brain in your head and recover after that too. But the unbearable hallucinations have ceased, and have now reduced themselves to a simple nightmare.

The doctor permitted van Gogh a few hours' visit to his home. The trip seemed to do him good. Shortly afterward, lulled by what appeared to be a complete recovery, the doctor discharged the artist from the hospital. He had only to visit and have his wound dressed occasionally. Van Gogh told his brother he had no more fear of another attack of irrationality, for he had been sleeping well.

Unfortunately, peace was not his for long. On returning home, he learned that the owner of the yellow house had rented it to someone else. Van Gogh would have to leave when his lease expired.

Moreover, van Gogh had learned nothing from Gauguin's careful handling of their money, and he suddenly found himself without funds. Once more he had to go without eating. Van Gogh was sane enough to realize that doing so might have an adverse effect on him. He warned the doctor. "For certain reasons I shall probably fast for a week. If this should affect me, do not think I have gone mad again!"

The artist got through the week successfully. He worked well and suffered no fresh attack. Unable to find models to sit for him, van Gogh continued to make self-portraits and painted the famous *Portrait of the Artist with Bandaged Ear*. He discovered that people, amused by the madman among them, were again laughing and talking about him, not caring whether he heard them. Certainly, he expected that news of his troubles would have spread, but he did not know how they could say he was mad, when he had been discharged from the hospital. One girl whom he knew slightly told him not to worry. "Everybody here is a bit mad," she said. "It is the mistral and the sun." The postman who delivered his mail became friendly and even posed for him. This sympathy comforted him, and his tensions relaxed a little. He preferred to believe that the climate made everybody a little crazy than to dwell on his fear of losing his sanity for good.

He wrote:

We are nothing but links in a chain. Old Gauguin and I at bottom understand each other, and if we are a bit mad what of it? Aren't we also thorough artists enough to contradict suspicions on that head by what we say with the brush? What it proves once more is that worldly ambition and fame pass away, but the human heart beats the same, in as perfect sympathy with the past of our buried forefathers as with the generation to come.

Van Gogh seldom left the house without encountering some children—and adults too—who jeered at him on the streets, and his hallucinations came back. He began to believe that people were joining together to poison him, even accusing strangers on the streets as well as those who mocked him. He could not sleep, afraid that if he did someone would enter the house and tamper with his food. All night long he padded up and down the stairs, in and out of the rooms. Unfortunately, for some reason or other, word of these developments did not reach his doctor.

By February he was again in the hospital. Mercifully, this attack seemed to pass quickly, and at the end of the month he was back at the yellow house again.

Once more van Gogh was the target of hatred and prejudice. Some feared him, others followed him on the streets out of curiosity, calling insults at him and telling him to go away from their town. People actually pursued him to his house and peered in at the windows. Boys even climbed to the upper story to look in, curious about what the madman might be doing. Finally, van Gogh rushed to his windows, threw them open, and screamed horribly at his tormentors to leave him alone and in peace.

The artist was forced from his home and taken again to the hospital. The police could not allow such a dangerous man free in the town, in view of the many complaints about him. He was locked in his room—alone. Screaming, he tried to drown the voices of the townspeople ringing in his ears. He wished to die. He recovered, however, though not without a great struggle. The doctor marveled that a man who had abused his health so could recuperate so quickly. For several weeks he lay in bed, silent and motionless. He was sure that if he gave way to the desire to scream in his agony, they would lock him up permanently. While in the hospital van Gogh was not allowed to paint, nor was he allowed the comfort of smoking. All he could do was think—or try to—and he maintained a complete silence.

Theo's letters were full of anxiety. Why didn't Vincent write? What was happening to him? Van Gogh felt too ashamed to write. This misery caused by his illness was the only reward his brother's loving efforts brought him.

Luckily, a good doctor had been called in on van Gogh's case. Doctor Salles hated the injustice of mob behavior with a passion. He felt that the neighbors' unjust treatment of the artist had victimized him. There was little that Doctor Salles could do about their behavior, but he finally succeeded in getting the artist to speak. "If the police had stopped those people from crowding around my house and looking in at my windows as if I were some kind of freak, this would not have happened," van Gogh told him.

Doctor Salles relayed to Theo an account of the events. Large numbers of people had complained to the mayor, saying that his brother was "a dangerous public nuisance," and that he should be locked away. As a result, the mayor had ordered Vincent seized and taken back to the hospital.

Theo van Gogh wrote to the hospital and insisted that his brother be set free and allowed to go to his home. Vincent's friend, the artist Signac, was going to be near Arles, and Theo begged him to visit his brother and see what was happening.

At the hospital Signac found van Gogh's door unlocked. He also found the artist looking well and behaving quite normally. Signac insisted that van Gogh was not mad, and he took the unfortunate man to his home. The house was locked, but they forced their way in. Signac genuinely admired van Gogh's work,

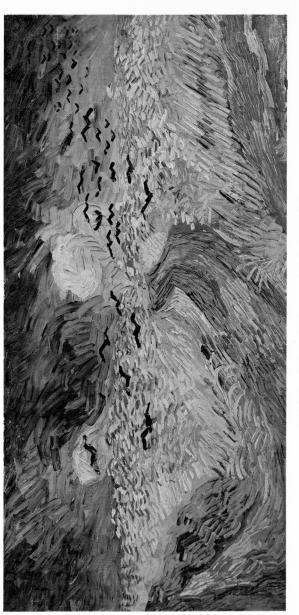

CROWS OVER THE WHEAT FIELDS
Auvers, 1890   Collection V. W. van Gogh, Laren

and his comments cheered the unhappy painter tremendously. Together they lugged back to the hospital all the paints and canvases they could carry.

In his report to Theo, Signac misjudged Vincent's true condition. He insisted again that van Gogh was not mad. Signac was used to artists acting strangely, and he thought van Gogh's behavior was not unusual. He blamed the ignorant people of the town. Faced with such treatment, who would not go a little crazy? If van Gogh only would eat properly and not drink too much, he would not be in this trouble. "Vincent had been working out in the fierce heat too much, then at night had been sitting alone drinking at a café, seldom taking the trouble to eat a decent meal. Such a routine is bad for anybody," he explained to Theo.

Painting in the hospital again van Gogh felt much better. None of the patients bothered him, especially when he took his easel outside. But he wanted to live in the yellow house, at least until he had to give it up in May. It was so close he could see it from the hospital. Doctor Salles and Doctor Rey discussed the matter, and neither of them felt the patient should go back to his home.

Theo van Gogh had little to suggest when the doctor told him of the problem. He thought perhaps Vincent could find another painter to live with. He told the doctors that his brother definitely could not go to live with their mother. "He has long since ignored convention. His dress and his peculiar manners mark him as different. People think he is mad. That doesn't bother me, but for our mother it would be impossible."

It was decided, finally, that van Gogh would move into rooms Doctor Rey found for him, a fair distance from the yellow house. The postman, Roulin, maintained his friendship with the artist, which was a comfort.

Sadly, van Gogh went with the doctor to pack his paintings and furnishings. Many of them would have to be stored. When the house was emptied, the artist looked around, heartbroken and despondent. The white walls were dusty; the red-tiled floor seemed to stretch into an eternity of emptiness. "I thought of how you have given me these things," he wrote to his brother. "Such brotherly love as you have, keeping me all these long years. Now I have to tell you this is the miserable ending of all the dreams I had."

"It is not the end!" Theo insisted strongly. "Rather it is a new beginning. Our regard for each other is worth more than all the worldly goods I shall ever possess."

Van Gogh, though hating to leave his house, was afraid to be alone. There were moments when he felt strong, sure his illness was over. Then dreadful thoughts entered his mind. What would happen if he did have another attack? Suppose he hurt himself? What awful things might he do to others? He had not forgotten how he had tried to harm Gauguin, and the thought terrified him.

At last van Gogh made a decision. He knew he

could no longer live in isolation, so he refused to move into the rooms. To Doctor Salles he said, calmly and quietly, "I am not fit to govern myself or my affairs."

Doctor Salles found a place for him in a village not far from Arles. At Saint-Rémy there was the old monastery of Saint Paul, which had been converted into an asylum. Doctor Peyron, who administered the institution, agreed to take him for one hundred francs a month.

And so in May, 1889, thirty-six-year-old Vincent van Gogh entered the asylum. There he hoped to find peace and quiet.

15 "WHAT'S THE USE?"

Theo was shocked by his brother's decision to remove himself from the world. He discussed the matter with his wife Jo, wondering if their marriage had anything to do with it. Johanna wrote to her brother-in-law herself, assuring him that she shared Theo's concern for him. Their marriage only added to the love surrounding him. It did not take away from it at all. The letter was a great pleasure to Vincent.

In the hospital, although he was not allowed outside, van Gogh was a privileged patient. He had two of the old monks' cells for his use, and from the barred windows he could see out over wheat fields. Beyond the wall around these fields a few cottages stood against a background of low hills.

But the black crows van Gogh painted in his landscapes of golden grain were harbingers of doom. In
1890, hospitals for the mentally ill were dreadful
places. The one at Saint-Rémy was an example of the
worst, and, at first, van Gogh was horrified. If the
patients fell to quarreling, they were left to settle
things by themselves. For recreation the inmates only
played checkers and the game of bowls. When the
weather was bad, they were confined to a stone-
walled room with one small stove and a few chairs.
On such days, with all the patients crowded together,
there was bedlam. The outlandish costumes worn by
some of the patients caused even van Gogh to raise an
eyebrow.

In such an atmosphere, it would not have been sur-
prising had the artist been pushed over the fine line
between sanity and insanity upon which he balanced
so precariously. Oddly enough, the opposite happened. He was a man who had suffered as much as a
man can and survive. He did not rave and storm at his
keeper; he made no fuss over the poor food. Instead,
he became quiet and gentle, helpful and kind to the
other patients. He finally was the kind of man he had
struggled to be all his life.

Surrounded by madness, van Gogh saw that it was
an illness like any other. Somehow, while at Saint-
Rémy, he lost his terror of it. Many of the patients had
moments when they were in control of themselves.
Then van Gogh talked with them, finding understand-

ing he would not have believed possible. Unlike people outside, the inmates did not find him strange or regard him as a freak.

And the artist started to paint again. "The idea of work as a duty is coming back to me," he wrote. There was good subject matter all around him, including the grubby buildings and the shabby garden with its pine trees. Van Gogh was astonished to find that, when he was outside painting, these supposedly mad people would look at his work, then leave him alone. How different, he thought, from the people in Arles who jeered and mocked me when I painted in the streets of their town.

In his work van Gogh's period of fascination with riotous color was over. He was painting now in softer, more natural colors closer to the real tones of the countryside. The abundant fertility of ripening grain and fruit and vegetables that surrounded him, he captured in bold strokes on his canvases.

Van Gogh had little comradeship in the hospital at Saint-Rémy, and he wondered if painting alone could sustain him. The women who took care of the patients had no use for him, considering him a burden they could do well without. One of them, however, did like his pictures and suggested they hang one in their retiring room. A chorus of horrified "No's" greeted the suggestion.

Once he made a trip into Saint-Rémy, and the experience unnerved him. The freedom made him feel dizzy, and he could hardly wait to get back to the security of the asylum.

By July, however, van Gogh seemed so much better that Doctor Peyron let him make a visit to Arles with his keeper Trabu. Passing the yellow house, which held happy memories, was difficult for him. When he visited the few people he had known who were kindly, van Gogh had mixed feelings of despair and eagerness. Some of these acquaintances talked of Gauguin. Despite the strain, the trip gave van Gogh a taste of life and freedom again, and when he got back to the hospital, his mind was full of hope, excitement, and some apprehension.

Shortly after his return, he was out painting *Quarry Near Saint-Rémy*. He was in a melancholy mood, and his subject and colors—red, green, and rusty brown—were soothing. Suddenly the awful mistral began to blow. Raging about him in a few minutes, the wind blew over his easel. He righted it and propped it up firmly with stones. As the wind grew stronger, it furiously flung up dust and small stones, which clung to the wet paint on his canvas. As the wind shrieked louder, reason fled, and dreadful pictures began to form in van Gogh's mind. Was the sound he heard the hateful wind shrieking, or was it the howling crowd from Arles coming after him again? Van Gogh writhed in agony—the wind tearing him outside, mental torment tearing him inside. Terrible screams ripped from his throat.

This attack was the worst yet. He had yelled so hard that his throat was bruised and sore, and several days passed before the artist was able to swallow anything. Despair and bad dreams gave him no rest. For several months he had been free of the nightmares, but now he seemed to suffer from them more than ever. Realizing that he would never be cured at Saint-Rémy, van Gogh began to loathe the place. He shut himself away in his cell, avoiding the other inmates. Viewing a reaper gathering grain from his barred window, he wrote, "In this reaper, fighting like mad under the blazing sun to finish his job, I see the image of death."

In a race against time, van Gogh painted all day long, desperately hoping to complete a series of works called *Impressions of Provence*. He believed that if he finished these paintings, his life would not have been in vain.

Theo urged him to come to Paris, suggesting that he might lodge with the painter, Pissarro. Pissarro was willing to have him, but his wife bluntly refused. Undoubtedly she thought having a husband and five sons all unsuccessfully dabbing paint upon canvas was bad enough without putting up with another penniless artist, especially one whom everybody knew was raving mad. Regretfully, Pissarro told Theo that he could not take his brother after all.

Pissarro knew someone else, though, who might help. Doctor Gachet, a heart specialist and a friend to many well-known painters, was interested in van

Gogh and in art. He said he would take him as a boarder, but van Gogh, still unsure of himself, resisted leaving Saint-Rémy. Although he had a few minor attacks, he was able to visit Arles. After Christmas, however, he began to feel that he could leave Saint-Rémy for good.

In the early months of 1890 Theo told him that Jo had borne a son and that the baby's name was Vincent. This news both pleased and appalled van Gogh. His fears passed when, in March, just before his thirty-seventh birthday, Theo reported that he had at last sold one of Vincent's pictures, *The Red Vine,* for four hundred francs. After ten years of work and suffering, van Gogh finally had earned some money. It was incredible to him.

In April he agreed to go to Paris. Packing his few belongings, he looked sadly around the place that had witnessed so much of his sorrow. "Ah," he cried, "if I could have worked without this accursed malady, what things I could have done!"

In mid-May, Theo met Vincent at the station in Paris. They spent several pleasant hours together in Theo's apartment. A lot of Vincent's work had been framed and hung on the walls; the rest was neatly stacked away. The artist was absorbed in studying the paintings he had done over the past ten years. He had never seen so many of them all together. Toulouse-Lautrec and his old friend Emile Bernard came to visit. Nobody said a word about Saint-Rémy and what had gone on there.

Paris palled quickly on van Gogh. He missed the clean air in the country and the bright colors of the South. The noisy traffic aggravated his nervousness. Finally, van Gogh could not stand Paris any longer, and he abruptly left the city, after promising to return and paint portraits of his brother and his family. Then he set out of find Doctor Gachet, who lived at Auvers, not far from Paris.

Van Gogh walked up the hill beside the River Oise to the doctor's house, a huge place with small windows, permitting little light inside. Doctor Gachet was at home, sketching.

Van Gogh did not care much for the gloomy house, but he liked Gachet's son and daughter. They took him to the backyard where there were poultry, cats, goats, and peafowl. The artist did not want to stay at Gachet's house, nor did he care for the inn the doctor suggested. Instead, he took a room in a cheaper lodging.

Exploring Auvers, van Gogh found it enchanting. At once he started painting views of the town. These pictures were different from those he had done at Saint-Rémy, and they showed that he was feeling better away from Paris. The colors were bright and lively.

Doctor Gachet insisted that the artist spend every Sunday with him. He hoped that if van Gogh had someone to talk with about his illness, a person also keenly interested in art, he would improve. And things went wonderfully well. Van Gogh felt very good and was satisfied with his progress. He learned that Gauguin was back in Brittany and wrote him, suggesting that he might join him there, so they could work together again. Gauguin was not enthusiastic about the idea.

Van Gogh did not have time to worry about Gauguin's indifference, though, because his brother and Jo arrived in Auvers to visit him. They were overjoyed to find him so well and doing such good work. Van Gogh was turning out some of his finest paintings. Gachet told Theo, "Every time I look at Vincent's pictures, I find something new. He is a giant. He's not only a great painter, he's a philosopher!"

Gachet was a good friend to van Gogh. Full of sincere enthusiasm, he was always praising his work. With this constant encouragement, the artist worked long and hard.

To his friend Bernard he wrote:

What excites me most about painting is the modern portrait. I want to create portraits which people a century hence will think look like apparitions. I'm not aiming at photographic likeness, but by using our modern knowledge and taste in color, to convey exaltation and character by the passionate expression of the face.

Things looked bright and promising in a way van Gogh would not have believed a few months earlier.

Then fate struck a blow from another quarter, destroying his hard-won serenity.

In Paris his brother's baby son was sick. As if this worry was not enough for a physically weak man, Theo was having great difficulties with his employers, again over the kind of painting he was urging on them. He tried hard to keep his troubles from his brother, but at last he had to let him know. If Vincent heard about them from other sources, he might think he was hiding things from him. Theo wrote him. "My consolation is that you have found your way."

The reassurances failed. Van Gogh could not stand the idea that the baby was his brother's first concern. It had always been he! His calmness vanished, and his recent peace ended. Say what they would, nobody really ever cared about him. "What can I do?" he asked in distress. He went to Paris, urging his brother to give up his job. The suggestion was absurd, and Theo, fretting about the baby, ill in the next room, was much too upset and worried to pay any attention. All these pressures were taking his brother's concentration and love away from van Gogh. He broke into a terrible rage when he considered his paintings in the apartment, stacked there uncared for and unloved.

Greatly disturbed, van Gogh went back to Auvers. Somehow he found Doctor Gachet extremely irritating now. He told his brother that Gachet was more unbalanced than himself. Every little habit of the doctor's began to loom so large in van Gogh's mind that, where once he had loved the man, he began to hate him. Gachet's sharp, firm tone when he spoke to him reminded him unpleasantly of Gauguin, and he abhorred Gachet's house. At the end of July, 1890, van Gogh exploded.

Visiting with Gachet in his study, van Gogh's mind began to grow dark. Casting furtive glances at his dusty canvases about the room of the man he had come to hate, he thought of his own neglected work in the Paris apartment. What was it all worth? . .

The confusion of his thoughts blinded him, and unable to distinguish between justice and injustice in his torment, he struck at the person whom he blamed for his sufferings. Action of any kind seemed to promise the only relief to the sick artist, and suddenly he pulled his revolver from his pocket and pointed it at Doctor Gachet.

"Vincent, what are you doing?" cried the doctor with alarm.

The sharpness of Gachet's voice reached the artist, and he felt ashamed and horrified about what he had intended to do. For a second time he had thought of killing someone. Where had his mind been? He turned and fled to his lodgings.

Van Gogh spoke briefly to another artist at the same place. "I can feel my life slipping away. I can't hold on any longer." Then he went to his room and wrote to his beloved brother:

You are more than a dealer at Corot's. Through me, you have helped to produce paintings which won't lose their meaning even if the world becomes a chaos. As for me, I'm risking my life for my work and my brain is beginning to give way. No matter. But you are *not* a mere tradesman. You can take *the part of humanity.*

He paused a few moments, then continued: "But what's the use?"

Van Gogh stood up and stuffed the unfinished letter in his pocket. He looked curiously at the gun in his hand. He had bought the revolver as a student at Cormon's art school. How long ago that time seemed. In his heart, the artist felt that his brother no longer needed him. The madness would strike again. Unable to control his actions, he would become a creature with no mind.

He left his room, walked up the road and into a field behind a château. Taking the revolver out of his pocket, he pointed it at his body and pulled the trigger. The bullet hit him in the abdomen, but he did not even lose consciousness. "Oh, God! Am I to fail even in this?" he cried. Clasping his hands over the wound, he staggered slowly back down the road, through the restaurant of the inn, and up to his room.

A short time later the landlord heard awful moans and groans coming from his tenant's room. He rushed up the stairs and, horrified, witnessed the scene. Van

Gogh lay on the bed, clothes soaked with blood, his face drawn in excruciating pain. He was smoking his pipe.

The landlord sent his daughter for Doctor Gachet. Aghast, Gachet dressed the wound as best he could. When he asked for Theo's address, van Gogh whispered hoarsely, "No, I will not give you his address. Theo is not to be disturbed. He has troubles enough."

Nevertheless, Gachet gave one of the artists staying in the village a note to take to the gallery next morning. Theo, about to leave for Holland to join his wife and child, wrote a few lines to Jo about the tragedy. "Don't worry, he has been worse and pulled through."

At Auvers, Theo found his brother still on his bed smoking his pipe. "Why, Vincent?" he sobbed. "Why?"

"Who would have imagined that life could be so sad?" van Gogh replied. "The burden of living is too heavy to bear alone, and I am alone. Once again I have failed."

Theo told his brother that his wife and child did not take away any of his love for him, but his words fell upon deaf ears. Vincent's will to live was gone.

The next morning, July 29, 1890, Vincent van Gogh wearily opened his eyes. "I wish I could die," he said. As though his prayer had been answered by a merciful God, a few moments later the thirty-seven-year-old artist was dead.

It was a hard death to end so hard a life.

EPILOGUE

The last episode in the story of these two remarkable brothers was about to begin. The tragedy of Vincent van Gogh broke his brother's heart.

Blinded by his grief, Theo somehow managed to get back home to Paris. Almost immediately he had a paralyzing stroke. Devotedly, his wife nursed him, but Theo van Gogh's mind gave way. Nevertheless, Johanna continued her tender care, and by the fall of 1890 she was able to take her husband with her to Holland. There Theo's sanity returned, but not his physical health.

In January, 1891, he died and was buried beside his brother in the churchyard at Auvers.

Badly in need of money, Johanna van Gogh packed all her belongings in the Paris apartment and returned to Holland. She took her husband's entire collection of paintings, which included more than two hundred of her brother-in-law's canvases. They were valued at 150 francs each.

Emile Bernard, Toulouse-Lautrec, and other friends were disturbed by Johanna's lack of means. "Why not sell the paintings?" they asked her. "At least you will get enough money to help you go on living."

"No," she said softly. "God does not demand futile sacrifice. They are gone, but this is only the beginning of their story. One day, I believe, Vincent's genius will be recognized. Theo's faith in him was too great, too sincere, for it to have been wrongly placed. I am sure the time will come—some day."

And the time did come. Johanna van Gogh lived to see her own faith justified. She lived to know that the genius who had caused her beloved husband so much pain was at last widely acknowledged and that his pictures were worth fortunes.

Emile Bernard, van Gogh's old friend, began to write articles about him and his work. Others took up the cause. Exhibitions were arranged. Toulouse-Lautrec, now in Theo's old position at the gallery, was able to draw attention to Vincent van Gogh's work. One day he was incensed to hear a slighting remark about van Gogh's paintings. His dark eyes blazing from behind thick spectacles, he drew his dwarfed body to its full height. There was a fierce dignity about his ludicrous frame as he challenged the disparager to a duel.

When Johanna van Gogh died in 1927, there was no bitterness in her heart.

As the controversy over van Gogh's genius raged, people began to see the artist's work in new light. Today it is a proud museum that can boast an original van Gogh in its collection.

Van Gogh had said: "I can't think people like Mauve cease to exist after death. Perhaps there will be something after that." He could not have known that his words about Mauve would be his own epitaph. But the beauty he left behind lives on, gladdening hearts as his was seldom gladdened while he lived.

LIST OF PAINTINGS AND DRAWINGS IN MUSEUMS IN THE UNITED STATES

Art Institute of Chicago, Chicago, Illinois
  Montmartre, Paris, c1886-87
  Men Drinking, Saint-Rémy, 1890
Baltimore Museum of Art, Baltimore, Maryland
  The Shoes, Paris, 1887
Barnes Foundation, Merion, Pennsylvania
  The Factory, 1887
  Bordello at Arles, 1888
Brooklyn Museum, Brooklyn, New York
  Cypresses, Saint-Rémy, 1889
Fogg Museum of Art, Cambridge, Massachusetts
  Self-Portrait (dedicated to Paul Gauguin),
    Arles, 1888
Herron Museum of Art, Indianapolis, Indiana
  Landscape at Saint-Rémy, 1889
Marion Koogler McNay Art Institute,
    San Antonio, Texas
  Women Crossing the Fields, 1890
The Metropolitan Museum of Art,
    New York, New York
  Cypresses, Saint-Rémy, 1889

Portrait of Madame Ginoux (L'Arlésienne),
Arles, 1888
The Minneapolis Institute of Art,
Minneapolis, Minnesota
Olive Trees, Saint-Rémy, 1889
The Museum of Art, Cleveland, Ohio
Road Menders—Boulevard at Saint-Rémy, 1889
Museum of Fine Arts, Boston, Massachusetts
The Postman Roulin, Arles, 1888
The Museum of Modern Art, New York, New York
Cottages at Saintes-Maries, 1888
Hospital Corridor at Saint-Rémy, 1889-90
Potato Eaters, Nuenen, 1885
Starry Night, Saint-Rémy, 1889
The Phillips Collection, Washington, D. C.
Entrance to the Public Gardens at Arles, 1888
Street Pavers, 1889
Houses at Auvers, 1890
Rhode Island School of Design,
Providence, Rhode Island
View of Arles, 1888
Collection of drawings
Toledo Museum of Art, Toledo, Ohio
Houses at Auvers, 1890

BIBLIOGRAPHY

Brill, Reginald, *Modern Painting and Its Roots in European Tradition*. London: Avalon Press, 1946.

Cheney, Sheldon, *Story of Modern Art*. New York: The Viking Press, 1941.

de la Faille, Jacob Baart, *Vincent van Gogh*. Paris: Hyperion Press, 1939.

Faure, Élie, *History of Art*. New York: Garden City Publishing Co., 1937.

Goldschneidre, L. and W. Uhde, *Vincent van Gogh*. Oxford and London: Phaidon Press Ltd., 1941.

Hanson, Lawrence and Elisabeth, *Passionate Pilgrim, The Life of Vincent van Gogh*. New York: Random House, 1955.

Hennessey, James Pope, *Aspects of Provence*. London: Longmans, Green and Co., 1939.

Lord, Douglas, ed., tr., *Vincent van Gogh, Letters to Emile Bernard*. New York: The Museum of Modern Art, 1938.

Meier-Graefe, Julius, *Vincent van Gogh*. John Holroyd-Reece, tr., New York: Harcourt, Brace & Co., 1933.

Rewald, John, *Post Impressionism, From van Gogh to*

Gauguin. New York: The Museum of Modern Art, 1962.

Stone, Irving, ed., *Dear Theo, The Autobiography of Vincent van Gogh*. New York: Doubleday and Co., 1958.

Thomas, Henry and Dana Lee, *Living Biographies of Great Painters*. New York: Garden City Publishing Co., 1940.

Tralbaut, Mark E., *Van Gogh, A Pictorial Biography*. New York: The Viking Press, 1959.

van Gogh, Vincent, *The Complete Letters of Vincent van Gogh*. Greenwich, Connecticut: New York Graphic Society, 1958.

INDEX

ABOUT THE AUTHOR

Born and educated in London, England, Alan Honour is now a citizen of the United States. During World War II he served for seven years in the Royal Air Force, and afterward lived in many European countries, spending some time writing film assignments in France and Italy. He has also traveled extensively in the Middle East and North and South Africa.

Now a resident of Richmond, Indiana, he has written several books for young people and has been awarded special citations by Indiana University for his contributions in that field.